THE Quotable A**hole

THE Quotable
A**hole

MORE THAN 1,200 BITTER BARBS, CUTTING COMMENTS, and CAUSTIC COMEBACKS

...FOR ASPIRING AND ARMCHAIR A**HOLES ALIKE

ERIC GRZYMKOWSKI

Adamsmedia
Avon, Massachusetts

Published by
Adams Media, a division of F+W Media, Inc.
57 Littlefield Street, Avon, MA 02322. U.S.A.
www.adamsmedia.com

ISBN 10: 1-4405-2565-X
ISBN 13: 978-1-4405-2565-0
eISBN 10: 1-4405-2907-8
eISBN 13: 978-1-4405-2907-8

Printed in the United States of America.

10 9 8 7 6 5 4 3 2 1

Library of Congress Cataloging-in-Publication Data
is available from the publisher.

This publication is designed to provide accurate and authoritative information with regard to the subject matter covered. It is sold with the understanding that the publisher is not engaged in rendering legal, accounting, or other
professional advice. If legal advice or other expert assistance is required, the
services of a competent professional person should be sought.
—From a *Declaration of Principles* jointly adopted by a Committee of the
American Bar Association and a Committee of Publishers and Associations

Many of the designations used by manufacturers and sellers to distinguish
their product are claimed as trademarks. Where those designations appear in
this book and Adams Media was aware of a trademark claim, the designations
have been printed with initial capital letters.

All interior illustrations © Jupiterimages Corporation.

This book is available at quantity discounts for bulk purchases.
For information, please call 1-800-289-0963.

DEDICATION

To my parents, who will proudly display this book
on their coffee table despite its title.

CONTENTS

INTRODUCTION

When our loved ones talk about their inane daily activities, we pay lip service to their incessant babble. When the barista screws up our coffee order, we convince ourselves that's what we really wanted anyway. And when our bosses ask us to work on the weekend, we smile politely and thank them for the opportunity to spend more time away from our families. In a world overflowing with awful drivers, taxes, crying babies, and street performers, most of us have learned to bite our tongues. But some a**holes aren't afraid to tell the rest of the world precisely what they think.

Throughout history thousands of a**holes have stood up in defiance of decorum and etiquette to denounce everything from friends and family to work and politics. You expect that behavior from characters like Winston Churchill, Joseph Stalin, and Mae West, but here you'll also find quotes from normally nice guys who lost their cool. (After all, if *you* find yourself screaming at the moron who cut you off in traffic, how can you expect high-profile figures like Walt Disney, Mahatma Gandhi, and Princess Diana to be perfectly perfect in every way?) So whether you want to join the ranks of these irreverent a**holes or just laugh in shock (and maybe even a little bit of awe) at the outrageously inappropriate words they've spouted off, you'll find what you're looking for here.

Political satirist P. J. O'Rourke said that you should "always read something that will make you look good if you die in the middle of it." *The Quotable A**hole* is not that book. But it is a place where you can embrace your dark side—and learn to love every overconfident, overblown, over-the-top a**hole comment that you'll ever need to know. Enjoy!

PART 1

DEALING WITH DICKS

I like long walks, especially when they are taken by people that annoy me.

—Fred Allen, American comedian

CHAPTER 1

FAMILY

Most people love their family members. They share your genetic material after all, and they shower you with unconditional love when times are tough. But just because a group of people are related to you doesn't mean you're thrilled with everything they do. Chances are, at one point or another, either your siblings or an errant uncle have shown up to an important event late, hungover, and wearing last night's clothes; your kids have screamed "I hate you!"; or your spouse has overdrawn your bank account . . . or at the very least forgotten to load the dishwasher. But the good news is that you are not alone. In fact, while it may seem like you are the first poor sap who had to deconstruct his pool table to make room for his mother-in-law, billions of people before you have dealt with family dicks. Most deal with the situation with a well-timed eye roll or a blowout that quickly blows over, but some a**holes take things to a whole other level with quotes like the following:

The problem with the gene pool is that there's no lifeguard.

—DAVID GERROLD,
AMERICAN SCIENCE FICTION
AUTHOR

If you don't believe in ghosts, you've never been to a family reunion.

—ASHLEIGH BRILLIANT,
AMERICAN CARTOONIST

I don't know half of

you half as well as I

should like, and I like

less than half of you

half as well as you

deserve.

—BILBO BAGGINS,
THE FELLOWSHIP OF THE RING

I don't have to look up my family tree, because I know that I'm the sap.

—FRED ALLEN,
AMERICAN COMEDIAN

Family love is messy, clinging, and of an annoying and repetitive pattern, like bad wallpaper.

—FRIEDRICH NIETZSCHE

Happiness is having a large, loving, caring, close-knit family in another city.

—GEORGE BURNS,
AMERICAN COMEDIAN AND ACTOR

Having children makes you no more a parent than having a piano makes you a pianist.

—MICHAEL LEVINE,
AMERICAN AUTHOR

A family is a terrible encumbrance, especially when one is not married.

—PRINCE PAUL, OSCAR WILDE'S
VERA, OR THE NIHILISTS

Santa Claus has the right idea—visit people only once a year.

—Victor Borge,
Danish comedian

We've been through so much together, and most of it was your fault.

—Ashleigh Brilliant,
American cartoonist

Some people stay

longer in an hour

than others can

in a week.

—William Dean Howells,
American author

While there certainly isn't a set of guidelines for grading fathers, you can determine a lot by their behavior. For example, a dad who takes his kid outside for catch and an ice cream is probably doing a pretty good job. But a dad who sends his son to the corner store with $5 and a note that says "A pack of Camels for me and M&Ms for the kid" might be doing it wrong. No matter where your dad falls on the spectrum, it's important to realize that every father has his faults, and those faults shape us into the men and women we grow up to be, but some people haven't been so polite about the issue. . . .

The place of the father in the modern suburban family is a very small one, particularly if he plays golf.

—Bertrand Russell,
British philosopher

To be a successful father, there's one absolute rule: when you have a kid, don't look at it for the first two years.

—Ernest Hemingway

Dad always thought laughter was the best medicine, which I guess is why several of us died of tuberculosis.

—Jack Handey,
American comedian

I never know what to get my father for his birthday. I gave him a $100 and said, "Buy yourself something that will make your life easier." So he went out and bought a present for my mother.

—Rita Rudner, American
actress and comedian

I remember the time I was kidnapped and they sent a piece of my finger to my father. He said he wanted more proof.

—Rodney Dangerfield,
American comedian

My father had a profound influence on me. He was a lunatic.

—Spike Milligan,
Irish comedian

Most mothers spend a lot of time kissing boo-boos and reading bedtime stories. But for some a**holes, dear old Mom can seem more like Mommie Dearest. If you want to use these words to talk about your own mom, feel free. But be careful if you decide to go this route. You know how your mom reacts when you do something as small as not calling her for a few weeks. We can only imagine how the following will go over.

Food, love, career, and mothers, the four major guilt groups.

—CATHY GUISEWITE,
AMERICAN CARTOONIST

The mother of three notoriously unruly youngsters was asked whether or not she'd have children if she had it to do over again. Yes, she replied. But not the same ones.

—DAVID FINKELSTEIN,
PROFESSOR AT THE GEORGIA
INSTITUTE OF TECHNOLOGY

My second favorite household chore is ironing, my first being hitting my head on the top bunk bed until I faint.

—ERMA BOMBECK,
AMERICAN HUMORIST

The lullaby is the spell whereby the mother attempts to transform herself back from an ogre to a saint.

—JAMES FENTON, ENGLISH POET

Damn you, vile woman! You've impeded my work since the day I escaped from your wretched womb.

—STEWIE GRIFFIN, *FAMILY GUY*

My mother's great. She has the major looks. She could stop you from doing anything, through a closed door even, with a single look. Without saying a word, she has that power to rip out your tonsils.

—WHOOPI GOLDBERG

There's something wrong with a mother who washes out a measuring cup with soap and water after she's only measured water in it.

—ERMA BOMBECK,
AMERICAN HUMORIST

At present time, there is no test you need to take or a form you need to fill out in order to produce children. Either through calculated planning or due to inexpensive prophylactics, millions of people become parents every year. And rest assured, somewhere down the line, their offspring will have something to say about it.

Parents are the last people on earth who ought to have children.

—SAMUEL BUTLER,
VICTORIAN NOVELIST

If you've never been hated by your child, you've never been a parent.

—BETTE DAVIS

Everybody knows how to raise children, except the people who have them.

—P. J. O'ROURKE,
AMERICAN POLITICAL SATIRIST

My parents only had one argument in forty-five years. It lasted forty-three years.

—CATHY LADMAN,
AMERICAN COMEDIAN

Adults are just obsolete children and the hell with them.

—DR. SEUSS

Parents often talk about the younger generation as if they didn't have anything to do with it.

—HAIM GINOTT,
ISRAELI CHILD PSYCHOLOGIST

Because of their size,

parents may be

difficult to discipline

properly.

—P. J. O'ROURKE,
AMERICAN POLITICAL SATIRIST

Children aren't happy without something to ignore, and that's what parents were created for.

—OGDEN NASH

There's no greater joy you can experience than holding a newborn child and knowing that this living, breathing extension of the heart was created through the miracle of life and love. This feeling usually lasts about fifteen seconds before said miracle spits up on your sleeve and needs a diaper change. In most cases, said child is handed back to his or her parents with a smile and a "Don't worry about it." But in some cases, that smile is followed up with a dry-cleaning bill and a comment like one of the following:

Always end the name of your child with a vowel, so that when you yell, the name will carry.

—Bill Cosby

Having one child makes you a parent; having two, you are a referee.
—David Frost,
British journalist

Raising kids is part joy and part guerrilla warfare.

—Ed Asner, American actor

My kids always perceived the bathroom as a place where you wait it out until all the groceries are unloaded from the car.
—Erma Bombeck,
American humorist

I married your mother because I wanted children; imagine my disappointment when you came along.
—Groucho Marx

A two-year-old is kind of like having a blender, but you don't have a top for it.
—Jerry Seinfeld

I knew I was an unwanted baby when I saw that my bath toys were a toaster and a radio.

—JOAN RIVERS

Before I got married, I had six theories about bringing up children; now I have six children and no theories.

—JOHN WILMOT, ENGLISH POET

If you wonder where your child left his roller skates, try walking around the house in the dark.

—LEOPOLD FECHTNER, AMERICAN AUTHOR

An ugly baby is a very nasty object—and the prettiest is frightful.

—QUEEN VICTORIA

Most children threaten at times to run away from home. This is the only thing that keeps some parents going.

—PHYLLIS DILLER, AMERICAN COMEDIAN AND ACTRESS

Human beings are the only creatures on earth that allow their children to come back home.

—BILL COSBY

Never raise your hand to your children—it leaves your midsection unprotected.

—ROBERT ORBEN, AMERICAN MAGICIAN AND COMEDIAN

Contraceptives should be used on every conceivable occasion.

—Spike Milligan, Irish comedian

I never met a kid

I liked.

—W. C. Fields

No single convention has spawned such bitter hatred as the concept of in-laws, and rightfully so. It's bad enough when a blood relative asks for a favor, but few things make the blood boil more than when your mother-in-law wants to join you on your anniversary weekend away or your father-in-law insists that he can fix your car better than your well-trained auto mechanic. And while you can't say no, there are certainly plenty of other things you can say—or at least think—while you set your mechanic's number to speed dial.

A relationship with your father-in-law is tough. You need to prove you can stand up to him, while being respectful. It's like walking a tightrope, which by the way I can do, because I went to trapeze school.

—Phil Dunphy, *Modern Family*

Humor is always based on a modicum of truth. Have you ever heard a joke about a father-in-law?

—Dick Clark

I told my mother-in-law that my house was her house, and she said, "Get the hell off my property."

—Joan Rivers

American couples have gone to such lengths to avoid the interference of in-laws that they have to pay marriage counselors to interfere between them.

—Florence King, American novelist

Honolulu—it's got everything. Sand for the children, sun for the wife, sharks for the wife's mother.

—Ken Dodd, British comedian

I saw six men kicking and punching the mother-in-law. My neighbor said, "Are you going to help?" I said, "No, six should be enough."

—Les Dawson, British comedian

I should, many a good day, have blown my brains out, but for the recollection that it would have given pleasure to my mother-in-law; and, even then, if I could have been certain to haunt her—but I won't dwell upon these trifling family matters.

—Lord Byron

Of all the peoples whom I have studied, from city dwellers to cliff dwellers, I always find that at least 50 percent would prefer to have at least one jungle between themselves and their mothers-in-law.

—Margaret Mead

Adam was the luckiest man; he had no mother-in-law.

—Mark Twain

The only reason my mother-in-law wasn't on Noah's Ark was because they couldn't find another animal that looked like her.

—Phyllis Diller, American comedian and actress

When you think of grandparents, you may think of handknit sweaters and hot tea. Or porch swings and storytelling. But maybe, instead, you think of garrulous old men and women who don't know how to use the Internet and can't hear anything you have to say. But just because they can't hear doesn't mean you should say nasty things behind their backs ... like the following a**holes did.

The woman who tells her age is either too young to have anything to lose or too old to have anything to gain.

—CHINESE PROVERB

If I'd known I was going to live this long, I'd have taken better care of myself.

—EUBIE BLAKE,
AMERICAN JAZZ MUSICIAN

Old men are dangerous: It doesn't matter to them what is going to happen to the world.

—GEORGE BERNARD SHAW,
IRISH PLAYWRIGHT AND AUTHOR

I want to die in my sleep like my grandfather . . . Not screaming and yelling like the passengers in his car.

—WILL SHRINER,
AMERICAN COMEDIAN

Why do grandparents and grand-children get along so well? They have the same enemy—the mother.

—CLAUDETTE COLBERT,
FRENCH ACTRESS

The denunciation of the young is a necessary part of the hygiene of older people, and greatly assists the circulation of the blood.

—LOGAN P. SMITH,
AMERICAN WRITER AND CRITIC

Sometimes the only thing greater than spending time with the people you love the most is spending time without them. This may seem counterintuitive, but there's a lot to be said for solitude. Unfortunately, many of you have wives, and husbands, and pets, and girlfriends, and taxes, and children . . . things that will not wait until halftime. So when your relaxing evening is interrupted by a torrent of inane babble, you have two choices: Pause the game, collect your patience, and deal with the situation at hand, or follow in the footsteps of one of the following a**holes and throw out one of these quotes:

I don't know, I don't care, and it doesn't make any difference!

—ALBERT EINSTEIN

Sometimes I need what only you can provide: your absence.

—ASHLEIGH BRILLIANT,
AMERICAN CARTOONIST

I don't want to be alone; I want to be left alone.

—AUDREY HEPBURN

Men want the same thing from their underwear that they want from women: a little bit of support, and a little bit of freedom.

—JERRY SEINFELD

Failing to be there when a man wants her is a woman's greatest sin, except to be there when he doesn't want her.

—POPE PAUL VI

I feel so miserable without you; it's almost like having you here.

—STEPHEN BISHOP, AMERICAN
SINGER AND SONGWRITER

The right to be let alone is indeed the beginning of all freedom.

—WILLIAM ORVILLE DOUGLAS,
ASSOCIATE JUSTICE
OF THE UNITED STATES
SUPREME COURT

CHAPTER 2

FRIENDS

For the most part, friends are the family you wish you had. They listen to your problems, let you cry on their shoulders, and support you when you get into trouble. But although your friends may have your back, that doesn't mean that they don't test your patience. Sure, your buddy helped you move into your first apartment, but don't forget the time he got drunk at Thanksgiving dinner and told your kids they were adopted. You'd think that when all was said and done, most people would be nice to the people who stand by them through thick and thin. (After all, they know all about your secret collection of Star Trek memorabilia and your inappropriate obsession with Cyndi Lauper, and they can use this information to destroy you.) But, believe it or not, there are a**holes out there who throw caution to the wind and repay their friends with comments like the following:

I don't trust him. We're friends.

—BERTOLT BRECHT,
GERMAN POET AND PLAYWRIGHT

My friends? There are no friends.

—COCO CHANEL

It is in the thirties that we want friends. In the forties we know they won't save us any more than love did.

—F. SCOTT FITZGERALD

When a man laughs at his troubles, he loses a great many friends. They never forgive the loss of their prerogative.

—H. L. MENCKEN,
AMERICAN JOURNALIST

The holy passion of friendship is of so sweet and steady and loyal and enduring a nature that it will last through a whole lifetime, if not asked to lend money.

—MARK TWAIN

The statistics on sanity are that one out of every four Americans is suffering from some form of mental illness. Think of your three best friends. If they're okay, then it's you.

—RICHARD BACH,
AMERICAN AUTHOR

Men kick friendship around like a football, but it doesn't seem to crack. Women treat it like glass and it goes to pieces.

—ANNE MORROW LINDBERGH,
AMERICAN AVIATOR AND WIFE
OF CHARLES LINDBERGH

I notice my wife when she's on the phone with her friends. Man, they will share every intimate detail of their lives with each other. See, men, once we become friends with another man, we may never say another word to him, unless there's valuable information that needs to be exchanged. Things like, "Hey, Jim, your shirt's on fire."

—JEFF FOXWORTHY,
AMERICAN COMEDIAN

Brutal honesty is something that can really only be shared between two close friends. When your wife or girlfriend asks you if she looks fat, the last thing she wants is an honest answer. But if you can't trust your friends to tell you what they really think, then whom can you trust? They usually say what they mean—and vice versa. But you may still want to avoid throwing daggers like the following:

'Tis a great confidence in a friend to tell him your faults; greater to tell him his.

—Benjamin Franklin

You even called me stupid in your verse, and I'm almost agreeing, for where stupidity is involved, you are quite an expert, friend.

—Franz Grillparzer,
Austrian writer

He doesn't get ulcers—he gives them.

—Henny Youngman,
British comedian

It takes two people to ruin a perfectly good day. First a person who says something downright nasty about you, and second, a dear friend who makes sure you hear about it immediately.

—Unknown

Everyone has a right to be stupid. Some people abuse the privilege.

—Joseph Stalin

There's a great power in words, if you don't hitch too many of them together.

—Henry Wheeler Shaw,
American humorist

Sometimes I'm so sweet even I can't stand it.

—Julie Andrews

Working with Julie Andrews is like getting hit over the head with a valentine.

—Christopher Plummer,
Canadian actor

I don't need a friend who changes when I change and who nods when I nod; my shadow does that much better.

—Plutarch

He is one of those people who would be enormously improved by death.

—H. H. Munro,
British author who wrote
under the pen name "Saki"

You may not realize it when it happens, but a kick in the teeth may be the best thing in the world for you.

—Walt Disney

Nestled snuggly amid your closest allies lies a small cesspool of parasites colloquially referred to as frenemies. Part friend, part enemy, these are the friends you love to hate. You may never know why they harbor such ill will toward you, but rest assured they gather together to plot your downfall on the second Sunday of every month. However, some a**holes make the ballsy decision to throw that verbal dagger right in the face of their frenemies. If you decide to do the same, borrow one of the following to make the most impact.

Why don't you bore a hole in yourself and let the sap run out?

—Groucho Marx

Your father should have pulled out.

—John Wayne

Wise men talk because they have something to say; fools talk because they have to say something.

—Plato

The difference between a misfortune and a calamity? If Gladstone fell into the Thames, it would be a misfortune. But if someone dragged him out again, it would be a calamity.

—Benjamin Disraeli, former British prime minister referring to his successor, William Ewart Gladstone

"Be yourself" is about the worst advice you can give some people.

—Thomas L. Masson,
American author

I'd call him a sadistic, hippophilic necrophiliac, but that would be beating a dead horse.

—Woody Allen

If I found her floating in my pool, I'd punish my dog.

—Yoko Ono

No friendship, however strong, is immune to the little green monster of jealousy. Even if you've known your best friend since you were both in diapers, chances are, you're still going to throw up a little in your mouth when your buddy gets yet another promotion while you're boss still can't remember your name. But is the problem the jealousy itself, or the fact that most keep it pent up inside? The following a**holes certainly felt it was the latter.

Most people enjoy the inferiority of their best friends.

—Lord Chesterfield,
seventeenth century
British nobleman

Probably no man ever had a friend that he did not dislike a little.

—Edgar Watson Howe,
American novelist

If you cannot answer a man's argument, all is not lost; you can still call him vile names.

—Elbert Hubbard,
American writer

The chief excitement in a woman's life is spotting women who are fatter than she is.

—HELEN ROWLAND, AMERICAN JOURNALIST

Laughing at our friends, we avenge the disappointment they have caused.

—MASON COOLEY, ENGLISH PROFESSOR AND WRITER

It is very easy to endure the difficulties of one's enemies. It is the successes of one's friends that are hard to bear.

—OSCAR WILDE

Fail, and your friends feel superior. Succeed, and they feel resentful.

—MASON COOLEY, ENGLISH PROFESSOR AND WRITER

While not everyone can claim to have hundreds of friends, most people have at least a few—even if they are imaginary. With so many people entering into the social contract of friendship, it stands to reason there must be some benefit—even if that benefit is minimal. But what do a**holes like about their friends? How do they express their appreciation? Read on.

A good friend can tell you what is the matter with you in a minute. He may not seem such a good friend after telling.

—ARTHUR BRISBANE, AMERICAN NEWSPAPER EDITOR

'Tis the privilege of friendship to talk nonsense, and have her nonsense respected.

—CHARLES LAMB,
BRITISH AUTHOR

A true friend is one who overlooks your failures and tolerates your success.

—DOUG LARSON,
AMERICAN COLUMNIST

It is so pleasant to come across people more stupid than ourselves. We love them at once for being so.

—JEROME K. JEROME,
ENGLISH AUTHOR

It is one of the blessings of old friends that you can afford to be stupid with them.

—RALPH WALDO EMERSON

He's the only man I ever knew who had rubber pockets so he could steal soup.

—WILSON MIZNER,
AMERICAN PLAYWRIGHT

Whereas most people love other people and value their friendships, there are some crotchety, misanthropic a**holes out there who feel that the average friend is about as useful as a paraplegic in a three-legged race. And these curmudgeons aren't afraid to tell their "friends" what they really think of them.

His mother should

have thrown

him away and kept

the stork.

—MAE WEST

And if I had a gun, with two bullets, and I was in a room with Hitler, Bin Laden, and Toby, I would shoot Toby twice.

—MICHAEL SCOTT, *THE OFFICE*

Friends: people who borrow my books and set wet glasses on them.

—EDWIN ARLINGTON ROBINSON, AMERICAN POET

I lay it down as a fact that if all men knew what others say of them, there would not be four friends in the world.

—BLAISE PASCAL, FRENCH MATHEMATICIAN

One good reason to only maintain a small circle of friends is that three out of four murders are committed by people who know the victim.

—GEORGE CARLIN, AMERICAN COMEDIAN

It's a lot like nature. You only have as many animals as the ecosystem can support, and you only have as many friends as you can tolerate the bitching of.

—RANDY K. MILHOLLAND, AMERICAN CARTOONIST MOST FAMOUS FOR THE WEBCOMIC, *SOMETHING POSITIVE*

Show me a friend in need and I'll show you a pest.

—JOE E. LEWIS, AMERICAN COMEDIAN AND SINGER

Bury the carcass of friendship: It is not worth embalming.

—WILLIAM HAZLITT, BRITISH WRITER

Some friendships are so strong that the circular narrative of life finds both parties back in diapers, laughing uncontrollably at each other's flatulence. But alas, nothing is eternal, and even friends as close as these will someday be parted. However, for some a**holes, the death of a close friend is not a time for mourning, but instead one where they are finally free to say all the horrible, heinous things they've ever thought about the old bastard (may he rest in peace, of course) from day one.

I have never killed a man, but I have read many obituaries with great pleasure.

—CLARENCE SEWARD DARROW, AMERICAN LAWYER FAMOUS FOR HIS DEFENSE OF JOHN T. SCOPES IN THE "SCOPES MONKEY TRIAL"

Saying I apologize is the very same thing as saying I'm sorry. They're the same. Unless you're at a funeral.

—DEMETRI MARTIN, AMERICAN COMEDIAN

Fuck this "Don't speak ill of the dead" shit! People don't become better when they are dead; you just talk about them as if they are. But it's not true! People are still a**holes; they are just dead a**holes!

—IAN FRASER "LEMMY" KILMISTER, BRITISH HEAVY METAL MUSICIAN

I cannot forgive my friends for dying; I do not find these vanishing acts of theirs at all amusing.

—LOGAN P. SMITH, AMERICAN WRITER AND CRITIC

He is useless on top of the ground; he aught to be under it, inspiring the cabbages.

—MARK TWAIN

He makes a very handsome corpse and becomes his coffin prodigiously.

—OLIVER GOLDSMITH,
IRISH WRITER

Old age is—a lot of crossed off names in an address book.

—RONALD BLYTHE,
BRITISH WRITER AND EDITOR

He was a great patriot, a humanitarian, a loyal friend— provided, of course, that he really is dead.

—VOLTAIRE,
FRENCH PHILOSOPHER

I didn't attend the funeral, but I sent a nice letter saying I approved of it.

—MARK TWAIN

CHAPTER 3

ROOMMATES

Anyone who has ever lived with someone else knows that roommates can be hard to handle. Consider this: You move in with your friends thinking that living together's going to be all fun and games. They seem kind and considerate and normal at first, but then something changes and that clean, polite, quiet person you've known all your life morphs into someone who leaves dirty dishes in the sink, refuses to clean the bathroom, and wakes you up in the middle of the night with his Lil Wayne ringtone. Sound about right?

When the bloom is off the rose, most people get down to business and have the awkward "I'm moving out" conversation, but that's not how a**holes operate. Despite the fact that their roommates have access to their toothbrush—and know where they sleep— a**holes never take the path of least resistance and, instead, fight back against bad roommates with some bad behavior of their own. . . .

I don't need to pay a therapist to give me crap. I have a roommate that does it for free.

—Calista Flockhart,
American actress

It's really hard to be roommates with people if your suitcases are much better than theirs.

—Holden Caulfield,
The Catcher in the Rye

I couldn't give a rat's tutu about your emotional distress.

—Judith Sheindlin,
Judge Judy

I'm not the easiest person to live with. I'm kind of a slob. So for me to consider a roommate, it would have to be one of my sisters or something.

—Katie Holmes

I used to have a roommate, but my mom moved to Florida.

—Rick Moranis

You're fucking annoying, seriously, just shut the fuck up because no one likes you in the house.

—Snooki to Mike
"The Situation" Sorrentino,
Jersey Shore

I would rather spend an hour among the notorious than two minutes with the dull.

—Stephanie Barron, Jane
and the Unpleasantness at
Scargrave Manor

Let's be honest: If given the option, the average person would try to avoid having a roomie for as long as possible. This is because the average person has better things to do than update chore charts and divine how a completely bald roommate can clog the bathroom sink. Since that's not always possible, the only thing that allows us to coexist peacefully is mutually understood rules of etiquette.

These rules can range from a complicated list of criteria for organizing dishtowels to more simple things like not allowing your roommate's cat to pee in your bedroom if it can be avoided. Whether you set these ground rules up front or wait for problems to arise first, they are quite necessary for successful cohabitation. Of course, some of these rules—and the conversations necessary to set them—can get a little hairy. . . .

The high point of civilization is that you can hate me and I can hate you, but we develop an etiquette that allows us to deal with each other because if we acted solely upon our impulse, we'd probably go to war.

—STANLEY CROUCH,
AMERICAN POP CULTURE CRITIC

I'm not concerned with your liking or disliking me . . . All I ask is that you respect me as a human being.

—JACKIE ROBINSON

I may have faults, but being wrong ain't one of them.

—JIMMY HOFFA

The question is not whether I treat you rudely, but whether you've ever heard me treat anyone else better.

—PROFESSOR HENRY HIGGINS,
MY FAIR LADY

Etiquette means behaving yourself a little better than is absolutely essential.

—WILL CUPPY,
AMERICAN LITERARY CRITIC

Your lack of manners is only exceeded by your lack of manners.

—DALE CARNEGIE,
AMERICAN AUTHOR

Is there no respect of place, persons, nor time in you?

—WILLIAM SHAKESPEARE

In the animal kingdom, the most violent and aggressive member of the pack is also often the most insecure. The same can usually be said for roommates. Sure, your roommate may stomp her feet and paw the ground like she's about to charge when you leave dishes in the sink, but the truth is she's bluffing. Whether you sit her down and talk about the issues or you assert yourself as the dominant creature in the relationship, take a look at the following comments designed to put a crappy roommate in her place.

She is the kitchen wench and all grease, and I know not what use to put her to than to make a lamp from her and run from her by her own light.

—WILLIAM SHAKESPEARE

I'll explain and I'll use small words so that you'll be sure to understand, you warthog-faced buffoon.

—WESLEY,
THE PRINCESS BRIDE

He had delusions

of adequacy.

—WALTER KERR, AMERICAN
WRITER AND THEATER CRITIC

People sometimes say my jokes are condescending. . . . That's when you talk down to people.

—JIMMY CARR,
BRITISH COMEDIAN

Oh, yeah? Well the Jerk Store called, and they're running out of you!

—GEORGE COSTANZA, SEINFELD

I never miss an opportunity to congratulate someone on being humorous, even if unintentionally.

—CHRISTOPHER HITCHENS,
BRITISH AUTHOR

Having one or more roommates is a sad enough state of affairs without adding more people to the mix. Occasionally though, some roommates fill an otherwise peaceful void with the irritating presence of unwelcome houseguests. Eventually these guests will grow tired of using all your clean towels and find other people to mooch off. But Ben Franklin said, "Guests, like fish, begin to smell after three days," and chances are, this happens sooner if the houseguests aren't actually there to visit you. Fortunately, the following a**holes have set a precedent on how to take matters into your own hands.

Every guest hates the others, and the host hates them all.

—ALBANIAN PROVERB

Visitors are insatiable devourers of time, and fit only for those who, if they did not visit, would do nothing.

—WILLIAM COWPER,
ENGLISH POET

I always feel that I have two duties to perform with a parting guest: one, to see that he doesn't forget anything that is his; the other, to see that he doesn't take anything that is mine.

—ALFRED NORTH WHITEHEAD,
BRITISH MATHEMATICIAN
AND PHILOSOPHER

Offer hospitality to

one another without

grumbling.

—BIBLE, 1 PETER 4:9

Staying with people consists in your not having your own way, and their not having theirs.

—MAARTEN MARTANS,
BELGIAN FOOTBALLER

No guest is so welcome in a friend's house that he will not become a nuisance after three days.

—TITUS MACCIUS PLAUTUS,
ROMAN PLAYWRIGHT

If there's one universal truth about roommates, it's that they hate work of any kind more than anything else. If they spent one-tenth of the time doing chores that they spent finding ways to avoid them, the house would be spotless and you wouldn't want to challenge them to a circle of death match once a week just to get them to mop the kitchen floor. So while you may just roll your eyes and grit your teeth when you come home to find your roommate nestled amid a sea of pizza boxes and empty beer cans banging away on a video game controller, think about what a**holes may blurt out in the same situation.

You're a parasite

for sore eyes.

—Gregory Ratoff,
Russian director, actor,
and producer

Procrastination gives you something to look forward to.

—Joan Konner, American
journalist and author

Laziness is nothing more than the habit of resting before you get tired.

—Jules Renard,
French author

Useless as a pulled tooth.

—Mary Roberts Rinehart,
American author

Housework can't

kill you, but why

take a chance?

—Phyllis Diller, American
comedian and actress

There are lazy roommates and then there are stupid ones. Why else would they not put out the garbage that you bagged and left for them to take care of while you were on an overnight business trip? While there are countless reasons to hate the person or people you share a living space with, it is quite possible it isn't all their fault. But a**holes don't see that as a reason to keep their mouths shut.

To the uneducated, an A is just three sticks.

—A. A. MILNE

A word to the wise ain't necessary— it's the stupid ones that need the advice.

—BILL COSBY

Your birth is a mistake you'll spend your whole life trying to correct.

—CHUCK PALAHNIUK,
AMERICAN NOVELIST

You're slower than a herd of turtles stampeding through peanut butter.

—DILBERT, *DILBERT*

You couldn't get a clue during the clue mating season in a field full of horny clues if you smeared your body with clue musk and did the clue mating dance.

—EDWARD FLAHERTY,
AMERICAN AUTHOR

I'm the master of low expectations.

—GEORGE W. BUSH

Ordinarily he is insane. But he has lucid moments when he is only stupid.

—HEINRICH HEINE,
GERMAN POET

While he was not dumber than an ox, he was not any smarter either.

—JAMES THURBER, AMERICAN
CARTOONIST AND WRITER

He that voluntarily continues in ignorance is guilty of all crimes which ignorance produces.

—SAMUEL JOHNSON,
BRITISH AUTHOR

They never open their mouths without subtracting from the sum of human knowledge.

—THOMAS BRACKETT REED,
FORMER SPEAKER
OF THE HOUSE

A person is smart. People are dumb, dangerous, panicky animals and you know it.

—TOMMY LEE JONES

In a perfect world, the people you are unfortunate enough to share a space with would get along famously—or at least tolerate each other's presence. Instead, your less-than-perfect world is likely littered with passive-aggressive notes and one of humanity's worst inventions—house meetings. It may seem like a horrible idea to get together and share all the little quirks you can't stand about each other, and that's because it is a horrible idea. But for a**holes who don't take them too seriously, house meetings can certainly be entertaining, especially when they bring along their best insults for when the respectful conversation devolves into childish name-calling.

Do you mind if I sit back a little? Because your breath is very bad.

—DONALD TRUMP

You can think I'm wrong, but that's no reason to stop thinking.

—DR. GREGORY HOUSE, *HOUSE*

I never make the mistake of arguing with people for whose opinions I have no respect.

—EDWARD GIBBON,
BRITISH HISTORIAN

Don't look now, but there's one too many in this room and I think it's you.

—GROUCHO MARX

I won't insult your intelligence by suggesting that you really believe what you just said.

—WILLIAM F. BUCKLEY JR.,
AMERICAN CONSERVATIVE
AUTHOR AND FOUNDER OF *THE
NATIONAL REVIEW*

If the person you are talking to doesn't appear to be listening, be patient. It may simply be that he has a small piece of fluff in his ear.

—WINNIE THE POOH, *POOH'S
LITTLE INSTRUCTION BOOK*

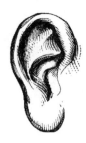

Madam, have you no unexpressed thoughts?

—GEORGE S. KAUFMAN,
AMERICAN PLAYWRIGHT

Buddhist monks possess an uncanny ability to ignore their surroundings and slip into a zen-like trance. Through years of meditation and intense training, they attain a spiritual oneness that protects them from life's myriad annoyances. Of course, the average monk doesn't have to live with a nudist, bagpipe-playing roommate. However, even a long-suffering roommate can take a lesson from the Buddhist monk and turn a blind eye when those annoying habits become overwhelming . . . or he can follow in the footsteps of the following a**holes and mutter the following under his breath.

When they discover the center of the universe, a lot of people will be disappointed to discover they are not it.

—BERNARD BAILY,
COMIC BOOK ARTIST

I would like to take you seriously, but to do so would be an affront to your intelligence.

—GEORGE BERNARD SHAW,
IRISH PLAYWRIGHT AND AUTHOR

Only a fool argues with a skunk, a mule, or the cook.

—HARRY OLIVER,
AMERICAN DIRECTOR

The unspoken word never does harm.

—KOSSUTH, HUNGARIAN
LAWYER AND POLITICIAN

Stop thinking, and end your problems.

—LAO TZU,
ANCIENT CHINESE PHILOSOPHER

You know what? Maybe there's a good reason donkeys shouldn't talk.

—SHREK, SHREK

The only fool bigger than the person who knows it all is the person who argues with him.

—STANISLAW JERSZY LEC,
POLISH POET

When tensions between roommates run really high and even attempts to take the high road fail, frustrated roommates can fall back on an old favorite: avoidance. While your lease does insist you pay rent on time, there's nothing in there that states you need to hang around with the people with whom you share a living space. But that doesn't necessarily mean you should declare open war on your roommates. The far easier, and less bloody, approach might be to just stay out of each other's way. However, some a**holes have trouble keeping their mouths shut and often break their silence to clue their roommates in on exactly what they're doing.

Constant togetherness is fine— but only for Siamese twins.

—VICTORIA BILLINGS,
AMERICAN AUTHOR

It is one of my sources of happiness never to desire a knowledge of other people's business.

—DOLLEY MADISON

People say conversation is a lost art; how often I have wished it were.

—EDWARD R. MURROW,
AMERICAN RADIO AND
TELEVISION JOURNALIST

Hermits have no peer pressure.

—STEVEN WRIGHT,
AMERICAN COMEDIAN

The stone often recoils on the head of the thrower.

—ELIZABETH I

Don't move! I want to forget you just the way you are.

—HENNY YOUNGMAN,
BRITISH COMEDIAN

Like all epic feuds, roommate disputes often reach a point where neither party remembers what the fight is even about. Did he forget to pick up toilet paper, or was it that he used your socks instead of buying more? The answer seemed important at first, but perhaps it's time to let bygones be bygones—an idea foreign to the everyday a**hole evidenced by the following commentary.

Don't walk away!

I'm trying to

apologize, you dumb

noodleloaf!

—CALVIN, *CALVIN AND HOBBES*

A mistake is always forgivable, rarely excusable, and always unacceptable.

—ROBERT FRIPP,
GUITARIST FOR KING CRIMSON

Drawing on my fine command of the British language, I said nothing.

—ROBERT BENCHLEY, AMERICAN
HUMORIST AND WRITER

You are a sad, strange little man, and you have my pity. Farewell.

—BUZZ LIGHTYEAR, *TOY STORY*

It is more fun to talk with someone who doesn't use long, difficult words but rather short, easy words like "What about lunch?"

—WINNIE THE POOH,
HOUSE AT POOH CORNER

CHAPTER 4

OTHER DICKS WHO PISS YOU OFF

Even if you are one of the lucky few to have been graced with a loving family, loyal friends, and a great roommate, you're still not immune from the hoards of obnoxious people out there waiting to ruin your day. Picture a zombie apocalypse, except the brain-hungry mutants have been replaced with double parkers, line-cutters, crackberry addicts, and people who chew with their mouth open.

While staying in your room crouched in the fetal position is a viable alternative to dealing with these dicks, it is by no means ideal. Eventually you will get hungry. So when you do finally venture out into the world, arm yourself with the following a**hole comments. This way, even if you only mumble these words over and over again in the safety of your locked car, you'll still feel like you're giving these dicks a piece of your mind.

Critics are like eunuchs in a harem; they know how it's done, they've seen it done every day, but they're unable to do it themselves.

—BRENDAN BEHAN,
IRISH AUTHOR

The trouble with her is that she lacks the power of conversation but not the power of speech.

—GEORGE BERNARD SHAW,
IRISH PLAYWRIGHT AND AUTHOR

Before you criticize someone, you should walk a mile in their shoes. That way, when you criticize them, you are a mile away from them and you have their shoes.

—JACK HANDEY,
AMERICAN COMEDIAN

Is that the way they drive in Tiananmen Square, bitch?

—ARI GOLD, ENTOURAGE

Let us be thankful for the fools. But for them the rest of us could not succeed.

—MARK TWAIN

Earth has its boundaries, but human stupidity is limitless.

—GUSTAVE FLAUBERT,
FRENCH NOVELIST

Nobody wakes up in the morning and thinks, "What a glorious day. I sure hope I run into a minefield of douche bags on my way to work!" But, unfortunately, this is precisely what is waiting for you out there. But your annoyance at your fellow man is by no means a detriment to your character; you should be commended for resisting the urge to run them all over with a Zamboni. Besides, you are certainly not alone; there are outspoken a**holes out there who aren't afraid to commend you for your irritability—or at least commiserate with you over it.

The road to truth is long, and lined the entire way with annoying bastards.

—ALEXANDER JABLOKOV,
AMERICAN AUTHOR

I just think she's a

vile, hideous human

being with no

redeeming qualities.

—BOY GEORGE ON MADONNA

I love mankind. It's people I can't stand.

—CHARLES SCHULZ, AMERICAN
CARTOONIST AND CREATOR OF
THE "PEANUTS" COMICS

Fools are without number.

—DESIDERIUS ERASMUS,
DUTCH THEOLOGIAN

Often it does seem a pity that Noah and his party did not miss the boat.

—MARK TWAIN

Some people are like Slinkies: not really good for anything, but you still can't help but smile when you see one tumble down the stairs.

—UNKNOWN

Dicks share a lot in common with children: They are immature, self-centered, and easily distracted. And just like children, the one thing they hate above all else is being ignored. So when a dick yells, pokes, prods, or stamps his feet, if you either walk away or take a note from the following a**holes, you'll be just fine.

To be insulted by you is to be garlanded with lilies.

—ARISTOPHANES

A gentleman will not insult me, and no man not a gentleman can insult me.

—FREDERICK DOUGLASS,
AMERICAN ABOLITIONIST
LEADER AND FORMER SLAVE

Listen to many, speak to a few.

—WILLIAM SHAKESPEARE

If you can't convince them, confuse them.

—HARRY S. TRUMAN

If you can't ignore an insult, top it; if you can't top it, laugh it off; and if you can't laugh it off, it's probably deserved.

—J. RUSSELL LYNES, AMERICAN
HISTORIAN AND AUTHOR

What you said hurt me very much. I cried all the way to the bank.

—LIBERACE

Rule number one, don't bother sucking up. I already hate you; that's not gonna change.

—MIRANDA BAILEY,
GREY'S ANATOMY

A wise man is superior to any insults which can be put upon him, and the best reply to unseemly behavior is patience and moderation.

—MOLIÈRE, FRENCH
PLAYWRIGHT AND ACTOR

Me think'st thou art a general offence and every man should beat thee.

—WILLIAM SHAKESPEARE

Do not speak, unless it improves upon silence.

—BUDDHA

While most dicks can simply be ignored, there are some who don't go away that easily. While your natural instinct may be to run and cower like a frightened child, some a**holes refuse to be intimidated and fight back with gems like the following.

Your ignorance cramps my conversation.

—ANTHONY HOPE,
BRITISH NOVELIST

When you go to the mind reader, do you get half price?

—DAVID LETTERMAN

I'll bet your father spent the first year of your life throwing rocks at the stork.

—IRVING BRECHER,
AMERICAN SCREENWRITER

Life's tough. It's tougher if you're stupid.

—JOHN WAYNE

I don't know anything about this man. Anyhow, I only know two things about him. One is, he has never been in jail, and the other is, I don't know why.

—MARK TWAIN

He is as good as his word—and his word is no good.

—SEAMUS MACMANUS,
IRISH AUTHOR

There are two insults no human being will endure: that he has no sense of humor, and that he has never known trouble.

—SINCLAIR LEWIS

I can't believe that out of 100,000 sperm, you were the quickest.

—STEVEN PEARL,
AMERICAN COMEDIAN

After a day when you've been flipped off, tailgated, and had your not-so-friendly waiter mess up your lunch order, maybe you wonder where all these everyday dicks came from in the first place. Well, anyone searching for an explanation for the prevalence of unapologetic, thoughtless jerks plaguing our society just has to turn back a few pages in the history books. When the Pilgrims landed on Plymouth Rock and started their relocation efforts of the indigenous people (read: genocide), we all cheered at the sudden appearance of fertile land at our disposal. When we started consuming all of the earth's natural resources to mass-produce motorized carriages, we all gave the thumbs-up and hopped on board. And when mindless, self-absorbed reality television "stars" appeared on every network, we venerated them as Gods instead of laughing them off the airwaves. So is it any surprise that the little punk who lives down the street thinks it's okay to fill your gas tank with sugar? And if you're not surprised, the following outspoken a**holes certainly weren't either.

The trouble with the world is that the stupid are cocksure and the intelligent are full of doubt.

—BERTRAND RUSSELL,
BRITISH PHILOSOPHER

People think it must be fun to be a super genius, but they don't realize how hard it is to put up with all the idiots in the world.

—CALVIN, *CALVIN AND HOBBES*

Expecting the world to treat you fairly because you are good is like expecting the bull not to charge because you are a vegetarian.

—DENNIS WHOLEY,
AMERICAN TELEVISION HOST

You take your life in your own hands, and what happens? A terrible thing: no one to blame.

—ERICA JONG,
AMERICAN AUTHOR

When you invite the whole world to your party, inevitably someone pees in the beer.

—XENI JARDIN,
AMERICAN TECH JOURNALIST

How sad it is that we give up on people who are just like us.

—FRED ROGERS

Never kick a fresh turd on a hot day.

—HARRY S. TRUMAN

Nature makes only dumb animals. We owe the fools to society.

—HONORÉ DE BALZAC,
FRENCH NOVELIST

People who think they know everything are a great annoyance to those of us who do.

—ISAAC ASIMOV, AMERICAN
SCIENCE-FICTION AUTHOR

It is impossible to defeat an ignorant man in argument.

—WILLIAM G. MCADOO,
UNITED STATES SENATOR

The one good thing about the number of dicks that you run into on daily basis is the fact that you realize how much better you are than them. And in fact, no matter how bad things get, there will always be an abundance of pricks, a**holes, and douche bags to remind you just how awesome you are. So before you wish for a plague to wipe out all the incorrigible dicks in the world, imagine how bad you'd feel without them. And just so you don't have to tell these morons what losers they are, the following a**holes have done it for you.

Take all the fools out of this world and there wouldn't be any fun living in it, or profit.

—HENRY WHEELER SHAW,
AMERICAN HUMORIST

He knows so little and knows it so fluently.

—ELLEN GLASGOW,
AMERICAN NOVELIST

Don't be so humble— you are not that great.

—Golda Meir, former
Israeli prime minister

Some folks seem to have descended from the chimpanzee later than others.

—Frank McKinney "Kin" Hubbard, American cartoonist

He has the attention span of a lightning bolt.

—Robert Redford

The true triumph of reason is that it enables us to get along with those who do not possess it.

—Voltaire,
French philosopher

PART 2

BYOB

Winston Churchill asked Lady Astor what disguise he should wear to her masquerade ball. She said, "Why don't you come sober, Mr. Prime Minister?"

CHAPTER 5

DRINKING

No one is sure exactly how our ancestors came across alcohol, but once they discovered its magical healing properties and ability to increase the attractiveness level of everyone around them, they spent far more time doing keg stands and far less time constructing spears. Flash-forward a few thousand years and little has changed. People still really love drinking and, for some, living close to a local watering hole is far more important than proximity to a functioning public school system. But where you find booze, you also find a**holes. There's just something about America's favorite pastime—and the lowered inhibitions that come with it—that brings out the worst in people.

To alcohol!

The cause of, and

solution to, all of

life's problems.

—HOMER J. SIMPSON, *THE SIMPSONS*

Why do they put the Gideon Bibles only in the bedrooms, where it's usually too late, and not in the barroom downstairs?

—CHRISTOPHER MORLEY, AMER-ICAN WRITER

It takes only one drink to get me drunk. The trouble is, I can't remember if it's the thirteenth or the fourteenth.

—GEORGE BURNS, AMERICAN COMEDIAN AND ACTOR

The problem with the designated driver program, it's not a desirable job, but if you ever get sucked into doing it, have fun with it. At the end of the night, drop them off at the wrong house.

—JEFF FOXWORTHY, AMERICAN COMEDIAN

I prefer to think that God is not dead, just drunk.

—JOHN HUSTON, AMERICAN ACTOR AND DIRECTOR

Drunks do not have friends, but accomplices.

—MASON COOLEY, ENGLISH PRO-FESSOR AND WRITER

I have made an important discovery . . . that alcohol, taken in sufficient quantities, produces all the effects of intoxication.

—OSCAR WILDE

Long conversations with pals when neither you nor they have had a drink can be a test of palship.

—P. J. O'ROURKE, AMERICAN POLITICAL SATIRIST

I think a man ought to get drunk at least twice a year just on principle, so he won't let himself get snotty about it.

—RAYMOND CHANDLER, AMERICAN NOVELIST

I drink, therefore I am.

—W. C. FIELDS, AMERICAN COMEDIAN

I have taken more out of alcohol than alcohol has taken out of me.

—WINSTON CHURCHILL

Of all the available options to get you tanked, none can eclipse the alluring appeal of good old-fashioned beer. It's cold, it's cheap, it's delicious, and it'll get you drunk. Unfortunately, it can also turn normal people whose company you may actually enjoy into raging, overconfident a**holes whom no one wants to be around. So it should come as no surprise that some of history's most notable public figures—as well as a few

obscure drunken jerk-offs—pulled a bottle out of their mouth long enough to wax poetic about God's amber gift to humanity.

Beer is living proof that God loves us and wants us to be happy.

—BENJAMIN FRANKLIN

Without question, the greatest invention in the history of mankind is beer. Oh, I grant you that the wheel was also a fine invention, but the wheel does not go nearly as well with pizza.

—DAVE BARRY, AMERICAN AUTHOR AND COLUMNIST

You can't be a real country unless you have a beer and an airline— it helps if you have some kind of a football team, or some nuclear weapons, but at the very least you need a beer.

—FRANK ZAPPA, AMERICAN ROCK MUSICIAN

A fine beer may be judged with only one sip, but it's better to be thoroughly sure.

—Czech proverb

Give me a woman who loves beer and I will conquer the world.

—Kaiser Wilhelm, German emperor

He was a wise man who invented beer.

—Plato

Payday came and with it beer.

—Rudyard Kipling

In a study, scientists report that drinking beer can be good for the liver. I'm sorry, did I say scientists? I meant Irish people.

—Tina Fey, American actress and comedian

When I heated my home with oil, I used an average of 800 gallons a year. I have found that I can keep comfortably warm for an entire winter with slightly over half that quantity of beer.

—Dave Barry, American author and columnist

Fat, drunk, and stupid is no way to go through life, son.

—Dean Vernon Wormer, Animal House

For those who lack the time and dedication necessary to get drunk off of beer, hard liquor can be a great alternative. There's something to be said for a drink that can kill you if you finish the entire bottle and, because it is more potent than beer, you can carry a small amount of hooch discreetly for occasions when alcohol is prohibited. But the thing about liquor is that even people who are low-key when throwing back a beer can turn into complete a**holes when drunk on whiskey sours or Long Island iced teas . . . especially if they're hiding their stash in a flask in their jacket pocket and pulling it out for nips during jury duty. Those dicks may say something like the following:

What whiskey will not cure, there is no cure for.

—IRISH PROVERB

I'll stick with gin. Champagne is just ginger ale that knows somebody.

—HAWKEYE, M*A*S*H

There is no such thing as bad whiskey. Some whiskeys just happen to be better than others. But a man shouldn't fool with booze until he's fifty; then he's a damn fool if he doesn't.

—WILLIAM FAULKNER,
AMERICAN NOVELIST

I need plenty of

wholesome nutritious

alcohol. The chemical

energy keeps my fuel

cells charged.

—BENDER, FUTURAMA

My grandmother is over eighty and still doesn't need glasses. Drinks right out of the bottle.

—HENNY YOUNGMAN,
BRITISH COMEDIAN

I should never have switched from Scotch to martinis.

—HUMPHREY BOGART, AMERICAN ACTOR

Nothing conveys an air of complexity and sophistication better than a nice glass of vino. But unfortunately, complexity and sophistication don't always walk hand in hand with good manners. It's not that wine drinkers are better than the rest of society; it's just that they are wealthier, smarter, and classier—or at least *they* think they are. There's just a sense of self-superiority afforded to wine drinkers that is not associated with other liquors . . . and that self-superiority breeds a high-class type of insufferable a**hole as evidenced by the snooty comments found here.

A man who was fond of wine was offered some grapes at dessert after dinner. Much obliged, said he, pushing the plate aside, I am not accustomed to take my wine in pills.

—JEAN ANTHELME BRILLAT-SAVARIN, FRENCH LAWYER AND POLITICIAN

When the wine goes in, strange things come out.

—JOHANN CHRISTOPH FRIEDRICH VON SCHILLER, GERMAN POET

I will not be as those who spend the day in complaining of headache, and the night in drinking the wine that gives it.

—JOHANN WOLFGANG VON GOETHE, GERMAN AUTHOR

Some weasel took the cork out of my lunch.

—W. C. FIELDS, AMERICAN COMEDIAN

From wine what sudden friendship springs!

—JOHN GAY, BRITISH POET

After God, long live wine.

—ROSALIA DE CASTRO,
GALICIAN WRITER

This is one of the disadvantages of wine: it makes a man mistake words for thought.

—SAMUEL JOHNSON,
BRITISH AUTHOR

This is the great fault of wine; it first trips up the feet: it is a cunning wrestler.

—TITUS MACCIUS PLAUTUS,
ROMAN PLAYWRIGHT

I cook with wine, sometimes I even add it to the food.

—W. C. FIELDS, AMERICAN
COMEDIAN

For some, drinking is a pastime. For others it's a vocation. But for a select few individuals, it's a way of life. Sure, you can think of them as pathetic degenerates, but perhaps you should stop to think about the sacrifices these a**holes are making on your behalf. For without them, to whom would you turn for a false sense of superiority?

I used to jog, but the ice cubes kept falling out of my glass.

—DAVID LEE ROTH

Being drunk is a good disguise. I drink so I can talk to a**holes. This includes me.

—JIM MORRISON

You're not drunk if you can lie on the floor without holding on.

—DEAN MARTIN

Always do sober what you said you'd do drunk. That will teach you to keep your mouth shut.

—ERNEST HEMINGWAY

What is it about a beautiful sunny afternoon, with the birds singing and the wind rustling through the leaves, that makes you want to get drunk?

—JACK HANDEY, AMERICAN COMEDIAN

Even though a number of people have tried, no one has ever found a way to drink for a living.

—JEAN KERR, AMERICAN AUTHOR AND PLAYWRIGHT

Whenever someone asks me if I want water with my scotch, I say I'm thirsty, not dirty.

—JOE E. LEWIS, AMERICAN COMEDIAN AND SINGER

Man, being reasonable, must get drunk; the best of life is but intoxication.

—LORD BYRON

Life is the boring bit between the hangover and the opening time.

—MICHAEL O'BRIEN, AMERICAN POET

If used responsibly and in moderation, alcohol can be a relaxing distraction from an otherwise hectic life. If used irresponsibly and to excess, alcohol can be so much more. While it's true that the end result of a night of binge drinking is often a morning spent wishing you'd never been born, many believe the consequences of excessive alcohol consumption are eclipsed by the myriad benefits. Among other things, alcohol makes you smarter, funnier, sexier, faster, and stronger. Although these enhancements generally only take place in the mind of the user, one should never underestimate the power of positive thinking.

Only Irish coffee provides in a single glass all four essential food groups: alcohol, caffeine, sugar, and fat.

—ALEX LEVINE, IRISH ACTOR AND MUSICIAN

Not all chemicals are bad. Without chemicals such as hydrogen and oxygen, for example, there would be no way to make water, a vital ingredient in beer.

—DAVE BARRY, AMERICAN AUTHOR AND COLUMNIST

I'd rather have a bottle in front of me than a frontal lobotomy.

—DOROTHY PARKER, AMERICAN POET

Alcohol is necessary for a man so that he can have a good opinion of himself, undisturbed by the facts.

—FINLEY PETER DUNNE, AMERICAN HUMORIST

Alcohol may be man's worst enemy, but the Bible says love your enemy.

—FRANK SINATRA

Sometimes when I reflect back on all the beer I drink, I feel ashamed. Then I look into the glass and think about the workers in the brewery and all of their hopes and dreams. If I didn't drink this beer, they might be out of work and their dreams would be shattered. Then I say to myself, "It is better that I drink this beer and let their dreams come true than to be selfish and worry about my liver."

—JACK HANDEY, AMERICAN COMEDIAN

A woman drove me to drink, and I never even had the courtesy to thank her.

—W. C. FIELDS, AMERICAN COMEDIAN

Despite all the evidence supporting alcohol as the greatest invention since the shot glass, there are a select few dicks who beg to differ. Using clever smoke-and-mirrors techniques like citing facts and conducting detailed studies, alcohol naysayers suggest prolonged consumption leads to liver disease, chemical dependency, and even heart problems. Whether you believe these snarky a**holes is up to you.

People who drink to drown their sorrow should be told that sorrow knows how to swim.

—ANN LANDERS

In my experience, you run into trouble when you ask a group of beer-drinking men to perform any task more complex than remembering not to light the filter ends of cigarettes.

—DAVE BARRY, AMERICAN
AUTHOR AND COLUMNIST

I think the warning labels on alcoholic beverages are too bland. They should be more vivid. Here are a few I would suggest: Alcohol will turn you into the same a**hole your father was.

—GEORGE CARLIN,
AMERICAN COMEDIAN

The chief reason for drinking is the desire to behave in a certain way, and to be able to blame it on alcohol.

—MIGNON MCLAUGHLIN,
AMERICAN WRITER

The really important things are said over cocktails and are never done.

—PETER F. DRUCKER,
AMERICAN SOCIAL ECOLOGIST

Health—what my friends are always drinking to before they fall down.

—PHYLLIS DILLER, AMERICAN
COMEDIAN AND ACTRESS

There are some lucky individuals blessed with stomachs so strong and blood so thick that there is almost no limit to the amount of abuse their bodies can take. Someone who gets a little woozy after his second appletini is not one of those people. But unlike his mutant counterpart, this guy understands an important concept that will serve him well: moderation.

So when your friend suggests you mix every type of booze in the bar into two glasses and see who can finish it first, pat yourself on the back for having the presence of mind to say, "You go first and tell me how it is." Sometimes it's better to listen to the gun-shy drunks who came before you rather than drinking first and asking questions later.

Beer is not a good cocktail-party drink, especially in a home where you don't know where the bathroom is.

—**Billy Carter, American businessman and younger brother to President Jimmy Carter**

If you drink, don't drive. Don't even putt.

—**Dean Martin**

Never accept a drink from a urologist.

—**Erma Bombeck, American humorist**

Instead of warning pregnant women not to drink, I think female alcoholics should be told not to fuck.

—**George Carlin, American comedian**

Worthless people live only to eat and drink; people of worth eat and drink only to live.

—**Socrates**

Be wary of strong drink. It can make you shoot at tax collectors—and miss.

—ROBERT A. HEINLEIN, AMERICAN SCIENCE FICTION AUTHOR

Some of the more dedicated drunks out there may be surprised to discover there are some out there who don't need to shove unfathomable amounts of tequila down their gullets in order to have a good time. For them, simple pleasures like taking a long walk or reading a good book are just as thrilling as seeing how many beers they can funnel before their insides become their outsides. While this type of lifestyle may be all right for some, it would be wise to listen to what some of the world's most notorious drinkers have to say on the subject before attempting it yourself.

I was sober for five years a long time ago and was just bored out of my tree.

—CHARLIE SHEEN

I feel sorry for people who don't drink. When they wake up in the morning, that's as good as they're going to feel all day.

—FRANK SINATRA

In 1969 I gave up women and alcohol and it was the worst 20 minutes of my life.

—GEORGE BEST,
IRISH FOOTBALLER

Moderation is a virtue only in those who are thought to have an alternative.

—HENRY KISSINGER,
AMERICAN DIPLOMAT

I distrust camels, and anyone else who can go a week without a drink.

—JOE E. LEWIS,
AMERICAN COMEDIAN AND
SINGER

I went on a diet, swore off drinking and heavy eating, and after 14 days I'd lost exactly two weeks.

—JOE E. LEWIS,
AMERICAN COMEDIAN AND
SINGER

Alcoholism is a disease, but it's the only one you can get yelled at for having. Goddamn it, Otto, you are an alcoholic. Goddamn it, Otto, you have lupus . . . one of those two doesn't sound right.

—MITCH HEDBERG,
AMERICAN COMEDIAN

After I quit drinking, I realized I am the same a**hole I always was; I just have fewer dents in my car.

—ROBIN WILLIAMS

I am not a heavy drinker. I can sometimes go for hours without touching a drop.

—NOEL COWARD, BRITISH
PLAYWRIGHT

CHAPTER 6
DRUGS

When we were kids, adults presented us with three unde-niable truths. First and foremost, Santa Claus was most definitely real. Second, eating watermelon seeds would surely cause one to grown in our stomachs. And last, but not least, drugs were bad.

Well, our older brothers and science have respectively disproved the first two truths, which brings into question the validity of the third. First off, as far as we knew, our parents had never tried drugs, so they were certainly in no position to make an informed decision on the matter. Sec-ond, there's the hypocritical fact that despite their insis-tence that drugs were bad, whenever we had a cough, they reached straight for the bottle of Robitussin.

In the years since then, hopefully you have come to your own conclusions about such important matters as drugs and the identity of a jolly fat man who breaks into people's houses. But if you still haven't made up your mind, there are plenty of outspoken a**holes out there who can help you formulate an opinion.

In the course of history, many more people have died for their drink and their dope than have died for their religion or their country.

—ALDOUS HUXLEY, BRITISH AUTHOR

I was banging seven-gram rocks and finishing them. Because that's how I roll. I have one speed, I have one gear: Go!

—CHARLIE SHEEN

I've tried everything. I can say to you with confidence, I know a fair amount about LSD. I've never been a social user of any of these things, but my curiosity has carried me into a lot of interesting areas.

—DAN RATHER

I used to have a drug problem; now I make enough money.

—DAVID LEE ROTH

Why is there so much controversy about drug testing? I know plenty of guys who would be willing to test any drug they could come up with.

—GEORGE CARLIN, AMERICAN COMEDIAN

I wouldn't recommend sex, drugs, or insanity for everyone, but they've always worked for me.

—HUNTER S. THOMPSON, AMERICAN AUTHOR AND JOURNALIST

The basic thing nobody asks is why do people take drugs of any sort? Why do we have these accessories to normal living to live? I mean, is there something wrong with society that's making us so pressurized that we cannot live without guarding ourselves against it?

—JOHN LENNON

I used to do drugs. I still do, but I used to, too.

—MITCH HEDBERG, AMERICAN COMEDIAN

I don't take drugs as an escape trick, like some cheap magician on a cruise ship. I take drugs to find gold, like a greedy prospector in the backcountry.

—RICHARD CLARK, THE AFRICAN SAFARI PAPERS

Few things in this world are as polarizing as the small, unassuming plant known as Cannabis sativa (a.k.a. marijuana). Some think it is a wondrous herb sent down from on high to help humanity deal with the trials and tribulations of life on Earth. Others, however, feel it is a vile substance that will destroy society if we let it take hold of our citizens. As with most things, if you fall in either extreme camp, you are almost certainly wrong. But that certainly never stopped anybody from preaching his or her point of view to anyone who will listen.

I think pot should be legal. I don't smoke it, but I like the smell of it.

—ANDY WARHOL

When I was a kid, I inhaled frequently. That was the point.

—BARACK OBAMA

Marijuana is not a drug. I used to suck dick for coke. Now that's an addiction. You ever suck some dick for marijuana?

—BOB SAGET, AMERICAN COMEDIAN

People say you can abuse pot. You can abuse cheeseburgers, too. We're not children. We're adults, and we are in control of our bodies for a limited period of time only, and we should experiment with it.

—JOE ROGAN, AMERICAN COMEDIAN, MARTIAL ARTIST, AND TELEVISION PERSONALITY

I smoked so much dope, I'm lucky I didn't turn into a bush.

—JOE STRUMMER, BRITISH MUSICIAN AND COFOUNDER OF THE CLASH

I used to smoke marijuana. But I'll tell you something: I would only smoke it in the late evening. Oh, occasionally the early evening, but usually the late evening—or the midevening. Just the early evening, midevening and late evening. Occasionally, early afternoon, early midafternoon, or perhaps the late-midafternoon. Oh, sometimes the early-mid-late-early morning . . . But never at dusk.

—STEVE MARTIN

There are really only two classifications of drugs: the ones that will ruin your life and the ones that will enhance it. Things like caffeine, Advil, and birth control pills fall into the latter section. And if you don't know which ones fall into the former, chances are, they already have.

But like most things, telling people to stay away from drugs is a sure-fire way to get them to try drugs. Humans are a curious breed after all, and some people just need to see for themselves.

Cocaine magnifies your personality. Yeah, but what if you're an a**hole?

—BILL COSBY

Opium teaches only one thing, which is that aside from physical suffering, there is nothing real.

—ANDRÉ MALRAUX, FRENCH
AUTHOR AND ADVENTURER

The best pitch I ever heard about cocaine was back in the early eighties when a street dealer followed me down the sidewalk going, "I got some great blow, man. I got the stuff that killed Belushi."

—DENIS LEARY

I'd always done a lot of [sniffing] glue as a kid. I was very interested in glue, and then I went to lager and speed, and I drifted into heroin because as a kid growing up everybody told me, "Don't smoke marijuana, it will kill you. . . ."

—IRVINE WELSH, SCOTTISH
NOVELIST AND AUTHOR OF
TRAINSPOTTING

Reality is a crutch for people who can't cope with drugs.

—LILY TOMLIN

Cocaine is God's way

of telling you that

you make too much

money.

—ROBIN WILLIAMS

I don't do drugs. I am drugs.

—SALVADOR DALÍ,
SPANISH SURREALIST PAINTER

There are many evil substances on this earth—oil, money, whatever is inside Cadbury Creme Eggs—but few things are as wrongly demonized as the poor, misunderstood recreational drug. Despite all the negative publicity drugs receive, millions of devotees continue to snort, smoke, inject, and eat their narcotic of choice to their hearts' content. And somehow, against all odds, the world continues to turn. Now this is not to say that drugs should not be taken with caution. Any substance that can make one believe he is the Jolly Green Giant deserves both our fear and respect. But maybe, just maybe, drugs are not transforming us into a society of a**holes. Perhaps the majority of us were just a**holes all along.

Drugs have done good things for us. If you don't believe they have, do me a favor: Take all your albums, tapes, CDs, and burn 'em. Because you know what? The musicians who made that great music that has enhanced your lives throughout the years . . . real fucking high.

—BILL HICKS,
AMERICAN COMEDIAN

I think religion is bad and drugs are good.

—BILL MAHER,
AMERICAN COMEDIAN AND
POLITICAL COMMENTATOR

A drug is neither moral nor immoral—it's a chemical compound. The compound itself is not a menace to society until a human being treats it as if consumption bestowed a temporary license to act like an a**hole.

—FRANK ZAPPA,
AMERICAN ROCK MUSICIAN

The arms of the drug police state are awesomely long. To drag a man back to jail for six months for nothing? He's not a danger to society.

—DALE GIERINGER, THE STATE
COORDINATOR OF NORML
(NATIONAL ORGANIZATION FOR
THE REFORM OF MARIJUANA
LAWS) IN CALIFORNIA

I've never had a prob-
lem with drugs. I've
had problems with
the police.

—KEITH RICHARDS

Did you know America ranks the
lowest in education but the high-
est in drug use? It's nice to be
number one, but we can fix that.
All we need to do is start the war
on education. If it's anywhere
near as successful as our war
on drugs, in no time we'll all be
hooked on phonics.

—LEIGHANN LORD,
AMERICAN COMEDIAN

Anyway, no drug, not even alcohol, causes the fundamental ills
of society. If we're looking for
the source of our troubles, we
shouldn't test people for drugs;
we should test them for stupidity, ignorance, greed, and love of
power.

—P. J. O'ROURKE,
AMERICAN POLTICAL SATIRIST

Of course, drugs were fun. And
that's what's so stupid about anti-
drug campaigns: They don't admit
that. I can't say I feel particularly
scarred or lessened by my experi-
mentation with drugs. They've
gotten a very bad name.

—ANJELICA HUSTON

While it may be difficult to
believe, there are some people out
there who think reality is just fine
and dandy the way it is. Despite
the availability of substances that
would let them taste music and
touch the color blue, they opt
to use their five senses the old-
fashioned (boring) way. And
all the power to them. It takes a
strong person to wake up every
morning and decide they are
going to make it through the day
without so much as a whiff of air-
plane glue to take the edge off.

The drug is really quite a remark-
ably safe one for humans,
although it is really quite a dangerous one for mice and they
should not use it.

—J. W. D. HENDERSON,
DIRECTOR OF THE CANADIAN
BUREAU OF HUMAN DRUGS,
HEALTH AND WELFARE

Every form of addiction is bad, no matter whether the narcotic be alcohol or morphine or idealism.

—Carl Jung

Don't do drugs because if you do drugs, you'll go to prison, and drugs are really expensive in prison.

—John Hardwick,
British director

I don't use drugs; my dreams are frightening enough.

—M. C. Escher,
Dutch graphic artist

You can turn your back on a person, but never turn your back on a drug, especially when it's waving a razor-sharp hunting knife in your eye.

—Hunter S. Thompson, American author and journalist

At first glance, lighting little white tubes to inhale cancerous smoke might seem a bit odd. Especially considering the ever-increasing price to do so. On closer inspection, however, there are plenty more dangerous things out there. Like base-jumping, shark wrangling, or testing unregulated medications for science. But you'd never know it by listening to the following a**holes.

I tried to stop smoking cigarettes by telling myself I just didn't want to smoke, but I didn't believe myself.

—Barbara Kelly,
Canadian actress

If cigarettes were bad, they wouldn't sell them everywhere.

—DICK SOLOMON,
3RD ROCK FROM THE SUN

A good cigar is like a beautiful chick with a great body who also knows the American League box scores.

—KLINGER, M*A*S*H

Like most people who smoked umpteen cigarettes a day, I tasted only the first one. The succeeding umpteen minus one were a compulsive ritual that had no greater savor than the fumes of burning money.

—CLIVE JAMES,
FALLING TOWARDS ENGLAND

It's easy to quit smoking. I've done it hundreds of times.

—MARK TWAIN

Smoking is one of the leading causes of statistics.

—FLETCHER KNEBEL,
AMERICAN AUTHOR

If I cannot smoke in heaven, then I shall not go.

—MARK TWAIN

What a blessing this smoking is! Perhaps the greatest that we owe to the discovery of America.

—ARTHUR HELPS, BRITISH
HISTORIAN AND NOVELIST

There are some circles in America where it seems to be more socially acceptable to carry a handgun than a packet of cigarettes.

—KATHARINE WHITEHORN,
BRITISH COLUMNIST

I'm glad I don't have to explain to a man from Mars why each day I set fire to dozens of little pieces of paper, and then put them in my mouth.

—MIGNON MCLAUGHLIN,
AMERICAN WRITER

There is one important point to make about drugs, and that is this: There are no elderly junkies. A life of excessive drug use does take its toll, and even the most hardened partier will eventually be forced to give up the rock star lifestyle and retreat to less destructive hobbies. Like snake charming.

While staying clean is by no means a simple task, you can take comfort in the fact that plenty of people have made a go at it before you. Some with more success than others.

I said stay off the crack, and I still think that's pretty good advice, unless you can manage it socially. If you can manage it socially, then go for it, but not a lot of people can, you know?

—Charlie Sheen

Avoid all needle drugs—the only dope worth shooting is Richard Nixon.

—Abbie Hoffman, cofounder of the Youth International Party

If we can get them to understand that saying no to drugs is rebelling against their parents and the generations of the past, we'd make it an enormous success.

—John Van de Kamp, American politician

All drugs of any interest to any moderately intelligent person in America are now illegal.

—THOMAS SZASZ, HUNGARIAN
PSYCHIATRIST AND PROFESSOR

Nothing makes it easier to resist temptation than a proper bringing-up, a sound set of values—and witnesses.

—FRANKLIN P. JONES,
AMERICAN AUTHOR

I only get ill when I give up drugs.

—KEITH RICHARDS

Those who flee temptation generally leave a forwarding address.

—LANE OLINGHOUSE,
AMERICAN AUTHOR

CHAPTER 7

A NIGHT ON THE TOWN

It takes a certain breed of individual to dedicate him or herself entirely to the pursuit of excessive partying. First and foremost, it requires a complete and utter disregard for personal safety and well-being. You'd have to be the type of person who hears about a bar downtown that features a mechanical bull surrounded by a viper pit and think, I need to be there!

Second, while not required, it is helpful to possess a distorted concept of right and wrong. Epic partiers realize that getting wasted and stealing a bulldozer to liberate all the monkeys at the zoo may not be the best idea in the world, but they also realize that if you want to stage an all-monkey fashion show, you're going to have to cut some corners.

Luckily you don't need to stage an all-night bender to see the appeal of that sort of lifestyle. Because if there's one thing history's most epic partiers enjoy more than anything, it's boasting about just how much harder they roll than anybody else.

One of the advantages of being disorderly is that one is constantly making exciting discoveries.

—A. A. MILNE

Turn the lights down; the party just got wilder.

—DAN RATHER

At a formal dinner party, the person nearest death should always be seated clos-est to the bathroom.

—GEORGE CARLIN,
AMERICAN COMEDIAN

Let us be lazy in everything, except in loving and drinking, except in being lazy.

—GOTTHOLD EPHRAIM LESSING,
GERMAN ENLIGHTENMENT
PHILOSOPHER

I've had a perfectly wonderful evening. But this wasn't it.

—GROUCHO MARX

Trouble defies the law of gravity. It's easier to pick up than to drop.

—JONATHAN RABAN,
BRITISH TRAVEL WRITER

I tell you, we are here on earth to fart around, and don't let anyone tell you different.

—KURT VONNEGUT

Going to a party, for me, is as much a learning experience as, you know, sitting in a lecture.

—NATALIE PORTMAN

By default, cruising around in a limo surrounded by half-naked groupies should be enough to make you a rock star. But truly epic partiers know you need to look good doing it, too. Unfortunately, the fashion industry is such a disjointed mess of incoming and outgoing trends, it can be difficult to determine what is actually en vogue at any given moment. Which explains why some fashionistas can get away with stapling raw meat to their bodies and calling it art. As any forward-thinking a**hole will tell you, the first rule of fashion is there are no rules.

People have told me about organized crime in the fashion industry, but I can't talk about that. I'm looking to stay alive.

—CALVIN KLEIN

Fashion as King is sometimes a very stupid ruler.

—E. T. BELL,
SCIENCE FICTION NOVELIST

I base most of my fashion taste on what doesn't itch.

—GILDA RADNER,
AMERICAN COMEDIAN

Fashion is an imposition, a reign on freedom.

—GOLDA MEIR, FORMER
ISRAELI PRIME MINISTER

Every generation laughs at the old fashions, but follows religiously the new.

—HENRY DAVID THOREAU

Fashion for the most part is nothing but the ostentation of riches.

—JOHN LOCKE,
BRITISH PHILOSOPHER

Fashion is a form of ugliness so intolerable that we have to alter it every six months.

—OSCAR WILDE

I buy expensive suits. They just look cheap on me.

—WARREN BUFFETT,
AMERICAN BUSINESSMAN

When I see a man of shallow understanding extravagantly clothed, I feel sorry—for the clothes.

—HENRY WHEELER SHAW,
AMERICAN HUMORIST

Nobody is quite sure what constitutes a party, but the general consensus is that one is made up of no fewer than five individuals gathered together in the pursuit of merriment. However, that number drops to four if alcohol is involved, three if there are drugs present, and one if both are combined. With such lax criteria, it's no surprise that the word *party* is attributed to everything from Mountain Dew–fueled gaming marathons to mandatory company ice cream socials. But regardless of the type of party, you can rest assured that there is somewhere else the majority of the attendees would rather be.

The cocktail party is easily the worst invention since castor oil.

—ELSA MAXWELL,
AMERICAN SOCIALITE

Nothing makes you more tolerant of a neighbor's noisy party than being there.

—FRANKLIN P. JONES,
AMERICAN AUTHOR

Cocktail party: A gathering held to enable forty people to talk about themselves at the same time. The man who remains after the liquor is gone is the host.

—FRED ALLEN,
AMERICAN COMEDIAN

She's afraid that if she leaves, she'll become the life of the party.

—GROUCHO MARX

Whenever, at a party, I have been in the mood to study fools, I have always looked for a great beauty: They always gather round her like flies around a fruit stall.

—JEAN PAUL RICHTER,
GERMAN AUTHOR

I like to go to parties where I know everyone. How are you going to have fun with people you don't know?

—MARY-KATE OLSEN,
AMERICAN ACTRESS

My evening visitors, if they cannot see the clock, should find the time in my face.

—RALPH WALDO EMERSON

Nothing is more irritating than not being invited to a party you wouldn't be seen dead at.

—WILLIAM E. "BILL" VAUGHAN,
AMERICAN COLUMNIST

Dessert is probably the most important stage of the meal, since it will be the last thing your guests remember before they pass out all over the table.

—WILLIAM POWELL,
AMERICAN ACTOR

Popularity is exhausting. The life of the party almost always winds up in a corner with an overcoat over him.

—WILSON MIZNER,
AMERICAN PLAYWRIGHT

Between the ambiguous hours of late and early, there is no shortage of temptations available for hedonistic partiers in search of a good time. No fetish or desire is too obscure or outlandish. If you are really into eating strawberry pancakes while watching one-armed bearded women do jumping jacks, then rest assured, there's a bar somewhere that will gladly provide that service. But don't go crying to them when you wake up in the morning covered in whipped cream and hating yourself.

All the things I really like are either immoral, illegal, or fattening.

—ALEXANDER WOOLLCOTT,
AMERICAN CRITIC

I prefer an interesting vice to a virtue that bores.

—MOLIÈRE, FRENCH
PLAYWRIGHT AND ACTOR

Do you really think it is weakness that yields to temptation? I tell you that there are terrible temptations which it requires strength, strength, and courage to yield to.

—OSCAR WILDE

Lead me not into temptation; I can find the way myself.

—RITA MAE BROWN,
AMERICAN AUTHOR

Yield to temptation. It may not pass your way again.

—ROBERT A. HEINLEIN, AMERI-
CAN SCIENCE FICTION AUTHOR

Why should not Conscience have a vacation?

—SAMUEL BUTLER,
VICTORIAN NOVELIST

How like herrings and onions our vices are in the morning after we have committed them.

—SAMUEL TAYLOR COLERIDGE

It is good to be without vices, but it is not good to be without temptations.

—WALTER BAGEHOT,
BRITISH WRITER

He has all the virtues I dislike and none of the vices I admire.

—WINSTON CHURCHILL

Everyone on earth gambles every single day; most just don't realize it. When you get behind the wheel of your car, you bet your life that none of your fellow motorists will cause you to lose it. When you go to your job, you wager a day's work that you won't get fired that day. Yet for some reason, when somebody wagers $10,000 that a little white ball will land in a little red hole, suddenly he's a degenerate. Say what you will about gambling for money, but at least all you lose are little green pieces of paper. That and a little dignity.

You cannot beat

a roulette table unless

you steal money

from it.

—ALBERT EINSTEIN

My luck is so bad that if I bought a cemetery, people would stop dying.

—ED FURGOL,
AMERICAN GOLFER

The only man who makes money following the races is one who does it with a broom and shovel.

—ELBERT HUBBARD,
AMERICAN WRITER

A dollar won is twice as sweet as a dollar earned.

—FAST EDDIE FELSON,
THE COLOR OF MONEY

The roulette table pays nobody except him that keeps it. Nevertheless a passion for gaming is common, though a passion for keeping roulette tables is unknown.

—GEORGE BERNARD SHAW,
IRISH PLAYWRIGHT AND AUTHOR

The urge to gamble is so universal and its practice so pleasurable that I assume it must be evil.

—HEYWOOD BROUN, AMERICAN JOURNALIST

My advice to the unborn is, don't be born with a gambling instinct unless you have a good sense of probabilities.

—JACK DREYFUS, AMERICAN BUSINESSMAN

The safest way to double your money is to fold it over once and put it in your pocket.

—FRANK MCKINNEY "KIN" HUBBARD, AMERICAN CARTOONIST

Most of the money you'll win at poker comes not from the brilliance of your own play, but from the ineptitude of your opponents.

—LOU KRIEGER,
PROFESSIONAL POKER PLAYER

Fortune, seeing that she could not make fools wise, has made them lucky.

—MICHEL EYQUEM
DE MONTAIGNE, FRENCH
RENAISSANCE WRITER

I've done the calculation and your chances of winning the lottery are identical whether you play or not.

—FRAN LEBOWITZ,
AMERICAN AUTHOR

If your picture of a wild Friday night finds you snuggling up with *The Lord of the Rings* trilogy drinking hot cocoa, you are not a badass. It's not that the illustrious works of J. R. R. Tolkien aren't exciting, but stories that end with " . . . and then I crashed the stolen Lamborghini into Mike Tyson's pool and escaped the KGB agents on foot" almost never begin with "So I got to the part where Frodo makes it to Rivendell . . ."

Never fear, though, as you can always live vicariously through these a**holes.

I'm tired of pretending like I'm not special. I'm tired of pretending like I'm not bitchin', a total freakin' rock star from Mars.

—CHARLIE SHEEN

Seven beers followed by two scotches and a thimble of marijuana and it's funny how sleep comes all on its own.

—DAVID SEDARIS,
AMERICAN HUMORIST AND
RADIO PERSONALITY

There's always some amount of gradual, slow-burning destruction over the course of partying.

—GAVIN DEGRAW,
AMERICAN MUSICIAN

If you go to a costume party at your boss's house, wouldn't you think a good costume would be to dress up like the boss's wife? Trust me, it's not.

—JACK HANDEY,
AMERICAN COMEDIAN

I never thought I was wasted, but I probably was.

—KEITH RICHARDS

The run I was on made Sinatra, Flynn, Jagger, and Richards look like droopy-eyed, armless children.

—CHARLIE SHEEN

If a single night out is awesome, then the equation for calculating vacation fun should look like this: (number of days off x awesome)^2. While rather eloquent, this simple equation fails to take into account certain mitigating factors that can alter the relative fun level, such as the number of children present on the trip, the relative proximity to flush toilets, and the likelihood you

will be shot if you leave the resort. As most of the following a**holes can attest, your time might be better spent taking the money you were going to spend on your trip, setting it on fire, and sitting in a comfortable chair for two weeks.

I hate vacations. If you can build buildings, why sit on the beach?

—PHILIP JOHNSON,
AMERICAN ARCHITECT

Babies don't need a vacation, but I still see them at the beach. I'll go over to them and say, "What are you doing here? You've never worked a day in your life!"

—STEVEN WRIGHT,
AMERICAN COMEDIAN

A vacation is what you take when you can no longer take what you've been taking.

—EARL WILSON,
AMERICAN COLUMNIST

A vacation is having nothing to do and all day to do it in.

—ROBERT ORBEN,
AMERICAN MAGICIAN AND
WRITER

By and large, mothers and housewives are the only workers who do not have regular time off. They are the great vacationless class.

—ANNE MORROW LINDBERGH,
AMERICAN AVIATOR AND WIFE
OF CHARLES LINDBERGH

No vacation goes unpunished.

—KARL HAKKARAINEN,
AMERICAN WRITER

Vacation: Two weeks on the sunny sands—and the rest of the year on the financial rocks.

—SAM EWING, RETIRED BLUE
JAYS OUTFIELDER

Part 3

Corporate Takeover

My father taught me to work; he did not teach me to love it.
I never did like to work, and I don't deny it. I'd rather read,
tell stories, crack jokes, talk, laugh—anything but work.
—Abraham Lincoln

CHAPTER 8

GETTING A JOB YOU'LL INEVITABLY HATE

When I was a kid, my parents bought me a game that involved putting little round pegs into little round holes. They did not do this because they enjoyed watching me see how far up my nose the pegs would go. Instead, they hoped that I might improve my motor skills and be capable of playing with the other kids in school without hurting myself. According to their master plan, I would then study hard into high school and avoid the temptations of sex, drugs, rock and roll, and fun of any kind, and earn the right to attend a private university. Four years and several hundreds of thousands of dollars later, I would finally be ready to achieve the be all and end all of human civilization—the 9–5 job. If I knew then what I know now, I would have told my dad to shove the peg game up his ass.

The truth of the matter is that there is no such thing as a fun job. Think about the guy who tastes new ice cream flavors for Ben & Jerry's. At first it was fun, but now he's 400 pounds and can't remember what his feet look like. But don't take my word for it. There are plenty of other a**holes who would rather slather themselves with peanut butter and go hunting for wolverines than spend five minutes in a cubicle.

All paid jobs absorb and degrade the mind.

—ARISTOTLE

If we guarantee employment for some, we jeopardize employment for everyone.

—ALBERT DUNLAP, AMERICAN CORPORATE DOWNSIZER

Life's disappointments are harder to take when you don't know any swear words.

—CALVIN, *CALVIN AND HOBBES*

President Bush is trying to put a positive spin on the latest bad economic numbers. Today he declared victory in the "War on Jobs."

—CRAIG KILBORN, AMERICAN ACTOR

Never wear a backward baseball cap to an interview unless applying for the job of umpire.

—DAN ZEVIN, AMERICAN HUMOR AUTHOR

If at first you don't succeed, remove all evidence you ever tried.

—DAVID BRENT, *THE OFFICE*

Never take a job where winter winds can blow up your pants.

—GERALDO RIVERA

Give a woman a job

and she grows balls.

—JACK GELBER, AMERICAN PLAYWRIGHT

Adults are always asking little kids what they want to be when they grow up because they're looking for ideas.

—PAULA POUNDSTONE, AMERICAN COMEDIAN

All I've ever wanted was an honest week's pay for an honest day's work.

—STEVE MARTIN

Thanks to some clever propaganda perpetuated by higher education, there are a few things you must do before you can even think about getting your first job. First you should borrow hundreds of thousands of dollars you don't have. Second, you must exchange that money, along with four years of your life, to obtain a piece of paper worth roughly sixty cents. Lastly, you must pretend as if you spent those four years studying rigorously instead of experimenting with drugs and alcohol. If you feel a little disenchanted with the process, you are certainly not alone.

I think everyone should go to college and get a degree and then spend six months as a bartender and six months as a cabdriver. Then they would really be educated.

—AL MCGUIRE, HEAD COACH FOR THE MARQUETTE UNIVERSITY MEN'S BASKETBALL TEAM

If you think education is expensive, try ignorance!

—DEREK BOK, FORMER PRESIDENT OF HARVARD UNIVERSITY

Education is what survives when what has been learned has been forgotten.

—B. F. SKINNER, AMERICAN BEHAVIORIST

Life is not divided into semesters. You don't get summers off and very few employers are interested in helping you find yourself.

—BILL GATES

It takes most men five years to recover from a college education.

—BROOKS ATKINSON, AMERICAN THEATER CRITIC

Education is an admirable thing, but it is well to remember from time to time that nothing worth knowing can be taught.

—OSCAR WILDE

Strange as it may seem, no amount of learning can cure stupidity, and formal education positively fortifies it.

—STEPHEN VIZINCZEY,
HUNGARIAN WRITER

A man who has never gone to school may steal from a freight car; but if he has a university education, he may steal the whole railroad.

—THEODORE ROOSEVELT

The purpose of a liberal education is to make you philosophical enough to accept the fact that you will never make much money.

—UNKNOWN

From the moment our parents asked us to clean up our toys for the first time, the vast majority of us have had a natural aversion to work. No matter how exciting the task may seem, there is always something better to do. Like biting your fingernails or silently counting to one billion, for example. Some might call this lazy, but the truth is the real a**holes are not the people who are hesitant to sit in a cubicle for eight hours a day. Rather, they're the people who pretend to like it there.

Doing nothing is very

hard to do . . .

you never know

when you're finished.

—LESLIE NIELSEN, CANADIAN
ACTOR AND COMEDIAN

I didn't want to work. It was as simple as that. I distrusted work, disliked it. I thought it was a very bad thing that the human race had unfortunately invented for itself.

—AGATHA CHRISTIE

I am a friend of the working man, and I would rather be his friend than be one.

—CLARENCE SEWARD DARROW, AMERICAN LAWYER FAMOUS FOR HIS DEFENSE OF JOHN T. SCOPES IN THE "SCOPES MONKEY TRIAL"

When people go to work, they shouldn't have to leave their hearts at home.

—BETTY BENDER, AMERICAN AUTHOR

Opportunity is missed by most people because it is dressed in overalls and looks like work.

—THOMAS EDISON

Play is always voluntary. What might otherwise be play is work if it's forced.

—BOB BLACK, AMERICAN ANARCHIST

I need so much time for doing nothing that I have no time for work.

—PIERRE REVERDY, FRENCH POET

Why should I have to WORK for everything?! It's like saying I don't deserve it!

—CALVIN, *CALVIN AND HOBBES*

The world is full of willing people. Some willing to work, the rest willing to let them.

—ROBERT FROST

More men are killed by overwork than the importance of this world justifies.

—RUDYARD KIPLING

If you can do a half-assed job of anything, you're a one-eyed man in a kingdom of the blind.

—KURT VONNEGUT

The ability to feed and clothe oneself is a desirable side effect of corporate life, but is the tradeoff really worth it? Anyone looking for a job should ask themselves if they'd rather have jury duty. If the answer is yes, maybe it's not the right way to go. But these people don't have anyone to blame but themselves. They are the ones applying after all; it's not like there is a draft. Perhaps, as these a**holes suggest, the real answer to the job crisis is to just stop looking for gainful employment. We might all be broke, but at least we'd be happy.

Work: a dangerous disorder affecting high public functionaries who want to go fishing.

—AMBROSE BIERCE,
AMERICAN WRITER AND AUTHOR
OF *THE DEVIL'S DICTIONARY*

Work is the source of nearly all the misery in the world. Almost any evil you'd care to name comes from working or from living in a world designed for work. In order to stop suffering, we have to stop working.

—BOB BLACK,
AMERICAN ANARCHIST

Work is a necessary evil to be avoided.

—MARK TWAIN

Work is a refuge of people who have nothing better to do.

—OSCAR WILDE

Dressing up is inevitably a substitute for good ideas. It is no coincidence that technically inept business types are known as suits.

—PAUL GRAHAM, BRITISH
PHOTOGRAPHER AND ARTIST

We don't have a lot of time on this earth! We weren't meant to spend it this way. Human beings were not meant to sit in little cubicles staring at computer screens all day, filling out useless forms, and listening to eight different bosses drone on about mission statements.

—PETER GIBBONS,
OFFICE SPACE

Corporations no longer try to fit square pegs into round holes; they just fit them into square cubicles.

—ROBERT BRAULT, AMERICAN
BLOGGER AND WRITER

Hard work spotlights the character of people: Some turn up their sleeves, some turn up their noses, and some don't turn up at all.

—SAM EWING, RETIRED BLUE
JAYS OUTFIELDER

There is no sure-fire method for securing a job, but most experts agree applying helps. Depending on the company, this process involves compiling all of your accomplishments into a coherent resume and possibly writing a detailed cover letter on why you would be the best receptionist in history. Similar to income taxes, there is a very low expectation that the information entered on either of these two documents is in any way factual. But before you blanket the job market with applications, it might be wise to check out what these a**holes have to say about them.

The closest to perfection a person ever comes is when he fills out a job application form.

—STANLEY J. RANDALL,
CANADIAN BUSINESSMAN

Avoid employing unlucky people. Throw half of the pile of CV's in the bin without reading them.

—DAVID BRENT, *THE OFFICE*

When you go in for a job interview, I think a good thing to ask is if they ever press charges.

—JACK HANDEY,
AMERICAN COMEDIAN

I'm doing everything I can to sabotage my career. It's a little thing called "fear of success."

—JON STEWART,
AMERICAN POLITICAL SATIRIST

When asked what they want to be when they grow up, most children aim high. President, astronaut, and marine biologist are all common aspirations. Fast-forward fifteen to twenty years and the bar gets a little lower. President becomes principal, astronaut becomes electrician, and marine biologist becomes aquarium cleaner. Depending on the job market, you may have to settle for roadkill remover or even less desirable positions like some of the dejected a**holes that follow.

If at first you don't succeed, try, try again. Then quit. There's no point in being a damn fool about it.

—W. C. FIELDS,
AMERICAN COMEDIAN

A lot of fellows nowadays have a BA, MD, or PhD. Unfortunately, they don't have a J.O.B.

—FATS DOMINO, AMERICAN R&B
AND ROCK AND ROLL PIANIST

Working for a federal agency was like trying to dislodge a prune skin from the roof of the mouth. More enterprise went into the job than could be justified by the results.

—CASKIE STINNETT,
AMERICAN AUTHOR

A great many people now reading and writing would be better employed keeping rabbits.

—Edith Sitwell, British poet

A life spent in constant labor is a life wasted, save a man be such a fool as to regard a fulsome obituary notice as ample reward.

—George Jean Nathan, American writer and editor

The trouble with the rat race is that even if you win, you're still a rat.

—Lily Tomlin

It's a shame that the only thing a man can do for eight hours a day is work. He can't eat for eight hours; he can't drink for eight hours; he can't make love for eight hours. The only thing a man can do for eight hours is work.

—William Faulkner

Going to work for a large company is like getting on a train. Are you going sixty miles an hour or is the train going sixty miles an hour and you're just sitting still?

—J. Paul Getty, American businessman

Men, take a moment to thank your penis. For without it, you would be earning 18.2 percent less money than you do now. (Women, the men are currently busying admiring their Johnsons; now would be a great time to stage a coup.) But aside from long-distance peeing, there aren't too many jobs that women can't perform as well or better than men. And while society could go on pretending that there isn't a problem, perhaps it's time to listen to what women have to say on the subject. Based on some of these comments, they might be just a tiny bit pissed that they're missing out on job opportunities just because they have lady parts.

Why is it men are permitted to be obsessed about their work, but women are only permitted to be obsessed about men?

—BARBRA STREISAND

For a woman to get half as much credit as a man, she has to work twice as hard and be twice as smart. Fortunately, that isn't difficult.

—CHARLOTTE WHITTON,
FORMER MAYOR OF OTTAWA

There are few jobs that actually require a penis or vagina. All other jobs should be open to everybody.

—FLORYNCE KENNEDY,
AMERICAN LAWYER AND EQUAL
RIGHTS ADVOCATE

The definition of women's work is shitwork.

—GLORIA STEINEM,
AMERICAN FEMINIST

The only jobs for which no man is qualified are human incubators and wet nurse. Likewise, the only job for which no woman is or can be qualified is sperm donor.

—WILMA SCOTT HEIDE,
AMERICAN AUTHOR AND
SOCIAL ACTIVIST

CHAPTER 9

WORKING FOR
THE MAN

Having a job means you've convinced some unsuspecting company to exchange forty hours of your time each week for green pieces of paper that you can later use to purchase goods and services. This scenario will play out every week until you are too old to realize how awful your menial tasks have become, or until you keel over and die—whichever comes first.

But don't start constructing that rubber band noose just yet; there is some hope. Now that you've secured a job, the hard part is over. If you can master the art of jargon and ass kissing, it's quite possible you will never be called upon to perform any tangible work for your entire career. Unless, of course, you are one of the select few saps who take pride in a hard day's work.

Like you, many of the a**holes in this chapter started their careers bright-eyed and ambitious. They showed up early, stayed late, and took care of everything that came across their desk. But slowly but surely they accepted the fact that the vast majority of their daily activities were utterly meaningless—and the liberation was exhilarating.

One of the symptoms of an approaching nervous breakdown is the belief that one's work is terribly important.

—BERTRAND RUSSELL,
BRITISH PHILOSOPHER

A good rule of thumb is if you've made it to thirty-five and your job still requires you to wear a name tag, you've made a serious vocational error.

—DENNIS MILLER,
AMERICAN COMEDIAN

Asking a working writer what he thinks about critics is like asking a lamppost how it feels about dogs.

—CHRISTOPHER HAMPTON,
BRITISH PLAYWRIGHT

Early to bed and early to rise probably indicates unskilled labor.

—JOHN CIARDI, AMERICAN POET

Work is of two kinds: first, altering the position of matter at or near the earth's surface relative to other matter; second, telling other people to do so.

—BERTRAND RUSSELL,
BRITISH PHILOSOPHER

Wednesdays are like Mondays in the middle of the week!

—LEE FOX WILLIAMS,
BRITISH ACTOR

Work is either fun or drudgery. It depends on your attitude. I like fun.

—COLLEEN C. BARRETT,
CORPORATE SECRETARY OF
SOUTHWEST AIRLINES

The ancient Romans had a tradition: Whenever one of their engineers constructed an arch, as the capstone was hoisted into place, the engineer assumed accountability for his work in the most profound way possible—he stood under the arch.

—MICHAEL ARMSTRONG,
AMERICAN BUSINESSMAN AND
FORMER CEO OF AT&T

Your business clothes are naturally attracted to staining liquids. This attraction is strongest just before an important meeting.

—SCOTT ADAMS,
AMERICAN CARTOONIST
AND CREATER OF THE
DILBERT COMICS

You don't make progress by standing on the sidelines, whimpering and complaining. You make progress by implementing ideas.

—SHIRLEY HUFSTEDLER,
FORMER SECRETARY
OF EDUCATION

If you love your job,

you haven't worked a

day in your life.

—TOMMY LASORDA,
AMERICAN MAJOR LEAGUE
BASEBALL PLAYER AND
MANAGER

Remember that intelligent, well-spoken person who hired you? He may look just like your boss, but rest assured he wasn't. Because the person you met in your interview surely knew how to use a computer, yet here you are watching your boss try to Google "revenue streams" from a fax machine. Every manager is different, but it generally only takes a few weeks before your fearless leader reveals himself or herself to be a bumbling idiot who ruins everything he or she touches. Don't believe it? Just be patient. You'll see.

If you think your boss is stupid, remember: You wouldn't have a job if he was any smarter.

—John Gotti,
American mobster

The world is divided into people who do things—and people who get the credit.

—Dwight Morrow,
United States senator

The longer the title, the less important the job.

—George McGovern

It is easy to fool yourself. It is possible to fool the people you work for. It is more difficult to fool the people you work with. But it is almost impossible to fool the people who work under you.

—Harry B. Thayer,
American businessman

Don't worry about people stealing your ideas. If your ideas are any good, you'll have to ram them down people's throats.

—HOWARD H. AIKEN,
AMERICAN COMPUTER ENGINEER

How much easier it is to be critical than to be correct.

—BENJAMIN DISRAELI, FORMER
BRITISH PRIME MINISTER

So much of what we call management consists in making it difficult for people to work.

—PETER F. DRUCKER,
AMERICAN SOCIAL ECOLOGIST

She has the answer to everything and the solution to nothing.

—OSCAR LEVANT,
AMERICAN MUSICIAN AND ACTOR

While there is certainly some important work being done out there in the world, chances are, it isn't being done by anyone in your office—least of all you. This is because, by and large, most work being completed at any given time is a complete and utter sham. And there's a very simple test to determine if your respective duties fall into this category. Step 1: Stop doing your job. Step 2: Wait two weeks. Results: If nobody noticed, your job is a sham. Once you have embraced that fact, you are free to meander along the path of mediocrity paved by the many a**holes who came before you.

As long as people will accept crap, it will be financially profitable to dispense it.

—DICK CAVETT, AMERICAN
TELEVISION TALK SHOW HOST

If I had $1 for every time someone came to me with not only a problem but also a possible solution to that problem, I'd have $6.

—BRIAN VASZILY, AMERICAN
MOTIVATIONAL AUTHOR

If you had to identify, in one word, the reason why the human race has not achieved, and never will achieve, its full potential, that word would be *meetings*.

—Dave Barry, American author and columnist

The easiest job in the world has to be coroner. Surgery on dead people. What's the worst thing that could happen? If everything went wrong, maybe you'd get a pulse.

—Dennis Miller, American comedian

Consultants have credibility because they are not dumb enough to work at your company.

—Scott Adams, American cartoonist and creater of the *Dilbert* comics

An expert is a man who has made all the mistakes which can be made in a very narrow field.

—Niels Bohr, Danish physicist

Business, that's easily defined; it's other people's money.

—Alexandre Dumas, French author

I know it's just a job they have to do, but sometimes I do wish they wouldn't.

—Princess Diana

A Mission Statement is a dense slab of words that a large organization produces when it needs to establish that its workers are not just sitting around downloading Internet porn.

—Dave Barry, American author and columnist

You can tell a lot about a person's job by the time between when they first sit down at their desk and when they take their first coffee break. The average is about thirty minutes, but for some workers this gap is so infinitesimal, if you blinked you'd miss it. But with a human parakeet for a boss and tasks so menial a trained hamster could perform them, who can blame them for shunning their responsibilities at every opportunity? Perhaps we should spend less time focusing on their less-than-stellar performance and more time focusing on what exactly it is about their work that sucks so hard.

Without work, all life goes rotten. But when work is soulless, life stifles and dies.

—ALBERT CAMUS,
FRENCH AUTHOR

I thought I could see the light at the end of the tunnel, but it was just some bastard with a torch, bringing me more work.

—DAVID BRENT, *THE OFFICE*

Oh, you hate your job? Why didn't you say so? There's a support group for that. It's called EVERYBODY, and they meet at the bar.

—DREW CAREY,
AMERICAN COMEDIAN, ACTOR,
AND GAME SHOW HOST

Why do people say they wish every day was Friday? If it was always Friday, we'd be here every freakin' day.

—ED BERNARD,
AMERICAN ACTOR

I'm going to insult a whole industry here, but it seems like TV is for people who can't do film. I'm not talking about actresses; I'm talking about lighting people. Lighting on TV is just so . . . it's sinful, it really is.

—KEVYN AUCOIN,
AMERICAN MAKEUP ARTIST

So I was sitting in my cubicle today, and I realized, ever since I started working, every single day of my life has been worse than the day before it. So that means that every single day that you see me, that's on the worst day of my life.

—PETER GIBBONS,
OFFICE SPACE

The sad reality of the working world is that it is not necessarily the most productive or most competent workers who get ahead: It's the ones that kiss the most ass. So continue to toil away in the hopes that your meager achievements will be rewarded, but your time would be far better spent remembering how your boss likes her coffee.

Employee of the month is a good example of how somebody can be both a winner and a loser at the same time.

—DEMETRI MARTIN,
AMERICAN COMEDIAN

Work is much more fun than fun.

—NOEL COWARD,
BRITISH PLAYWRIGHT

People who enjoy meetings should not be in charge of anything.

—THOMAS SOWELL, AMERICAN
ECONOMIST AND AUTHOR

It's no credit to anyone to work too hard.

—EDGAR WATSON HOWE,
AMERICAN NOVELIST

Work is accomplished by those employees who have not yet reached their level of incompetence.

—LAURENCE J. PETER,
CANADIAN AUTHOR

If you hand a last-minute assignment to a motivated employee who dutifully performs his or her job for eight hours a day, chances are, it will get done without a problem. Assign the same work to a lazy employee, however, and you might as well have asked him to tear down the Berlin Wall by 5 P.M.

It's not that the work is especially difficult. It's just that the average procrastinator would rather jump headfirst into an active volcano than run down to marketing to ask what color the new logo should be. So by all means, keep assigning work to these lazy a**holes. Just don't be surprised when it comes back half finished, or not at all.

Procrastination is like a credit card; it's a lot of fun until you get the bill.

—CHRISTOPHER PARKER,
BRITISH ACTOR

Accomplishing the impossible means only the boss will add it to your regular duties.

—DOUG LARSON,
AMERICAN COLUMNIST

Hard work is damn near as overrated as monogamy.

—HUEY LONG, FORMER
LOUISIANA GOVERNOR

I ain't sleeping. I'm just taking a good look at the insides of my eyelids.

—JONATHAN RABAN,
BRITISH TRAVEL WRITER

Anyone can do any amount of work provided it isn't the work he is supposed to be doing at the moment.

—ROBERT BENCHLEY, AMERICAN
HUMORIST AND WRITER

Whenever there is a hard job to be done, I assign it to a lazy man; he is sure to find an easy way of doing it.

—WALTER CHRYSLER,
AMERICAN BUSINESSMAN AND
FOUNDER OF THE CHRYSLER
CORPORATION

The reason why worry kills more people than work is that more people worry than work.

—ROBERT FROST

The brain is a wonderful organ; it starts working the moment you get up in the morning and does not stop until you get into the office.

—ROBERT FROST

The only thing that ever sat its way to success was a hen.

—SARAH BROWN,
AMERICAN ACTRESS

Somewhere between insufferable kissass and degenerate lazy a**hole lies the ideal employee. He knows when to say yes, but he also knows when to keep his mouth shut. He performs all the work that comes across his desk adequately and on time, but he certainly doesn't seek out any more once it's done. His zen-like mediocrity is a thing of beauty, and if you can find one of these at your office, you would be wise to take notes. If you can manage to do just enough work to look busy, but not so much that you actually are, your job might even become almost bearable. Maybe.

I want to share something with you: The three little sentences that will get you through life. Number 1: Cover for me. Number 2: Oh, good idea, Boss! Number 3: It was like that when I got here.

—HOMER J. SIMPSON,
THE SIMPSONS

If A equals success, then the formula is A equals X plus Y and Z, with X being work, Y play, and Z keeping your mouth shut.

—ALBERT EINSTEIN

By working faithfully eight hours a day, you may eventually get to be boss and work twelve hours a day.

—ROBERT FROST

Whenever you are asked if you can do a job, tell 'em, "Certainly, I can!" Then get busy and find out how to do it.

—THEODORE ROOSEVELT

Every person I work with knows something better than me. My job is to listen long enough to find it and use it.

—JACK NICHOLS,
AMERICAN GAY RIGHTS ACTIVIST

When things go wrong at work, as they inevitably will, the proper strategy could mean the difference between getting canned and getting promoted. At the end of the day, nobody really wants to know how to fix the problem. They want to know whom to blame.

In this predicament an employee only has two options: (A) Cowboy up and accept responsibility for the mistake or (B) roll over on the closest coworker with a pulse. This guy may be an a**hole, but at least he's an a**hole who still has a job.

Nothing is impossible for the man who doesn't have to do it himself.

—A. H. WEILER,
NEW YORK TIMES FILM EDITOR

I am not disposed to complain that I have planted and others have gathered the fruits.

—CHARLES GOODYEAR,
AMERICAN INVENTOR

Eagles may soar high, but weasels don't get sucked into jet engines.

—JOHN BENFIELD,
BRITISH ACTOR

The man who smiles when things go wrong has thought of someone to blame it on.

—ROBERT BLOCH,
AMERICAN NOVELIST

Executive ability is deciding quickly and getting somebody else to do the work.

—EARL NIGHTINGALE,
AMERICAN AUTHOR AND
MOTIVATIONAL SPEAKER

If work was so good, the rich would have kept more of it for themselves.

—DAVID BRENT, *THE OFFICE*

My job consists of basically masking my contempt for the a**holes in charge and, at least once a day, retiring to the men's room so I can jerk off while I fantasize about a life that doesn't so closely resemble hell.

—LESTER BURNHAM,
AMERICAN BEAUTY

I always arrive late at the office, but I make up for it by leaving early.

—CHARLES LAMB,
BRITISH AUTHOR

If you're gonna be late, then be late and not just two minutes—make it an hour and enjoy your breakfast.

—DAVID BRENT, *THE OFFICE*

I like work;

it fascinates me.

I can sit and look at

it for hours.

—JEROME K. JEROME,
ENGLISH AUTHOR

Work is the greatest

thing in the world,

so we should always

save some of it for

tomorrow.

—DON HEROLD,
AMERICAN HUMORIST

If your boss is getting you down, look at him through the prongs of a fork and imagine him in jail.

—DAVID BRENT, *THE OFFICE*

CHAPTER 10
GETTING FIRED

There are few things worse than sacrificing years of your life at a soul-sucking job, only to trudge into the office one day and discover a pink slip sticking out of your mailbox. But unlike other earth-shattering pieces of news, which result in five stages of acceptance, getting fired usually only results in two: Shock and anger immediately followed by a general, meh feeling that is difficult to describe. (It's kind of like discovering that your dog died, but then realizing he spent all his time biting your ankles and pooping on your carpet.) But no matter how you look at it, getting fired really sucks . . . as the bitter a**holes quoted throughout this chapter can attest.

I mean, there's no arguing. There is no anything. There is no beating around the bush. *You're fired* is a very strong term.

—DONALD TRUMP

Most people work

just hard enough

not to get fired and

get paid just enough

money not to quit.

—GEORGE CARLIN,
AMERICAN COMEDIAN

I don't know what else we can cut when we've already laid off all these people whose skills we could use right now.

—GREG MEFFERT,
DEPUTY MAYOR
OF NEW ORLEANS
DURING HURRICANE KATRINA

When we're unemployed, we're called lazy; when the whites are unemployed, it's called a depression.

—JESSE JACKSON, AMERICAN
CIVIL RIGHTS ACTIVIST

Be nice to people on your way up because you meet them on your way down.

—JIMMY DURANTE,
AMERICAN ACTOR AND MUSICIAN

You're fired! No other words can so easily and succinctly reduce a confident, self-assured executive to an insecure, groveling shred of his former self.

—FRANK P. LOUCHHEIM,
AMERICAN BUSINESSMAN

The bulk of the increase since 1998 is suicides by men who are middle-aged or older and have either been laid off or whose businesses have failed.

—MASAHIRO YAMADA,
JAPANESE SOCIOLOGIST

I am still in shock and awe at being fired.

—PETER ARNETT,
NEW ZEALANDER JOURNALIST

Recession is when a neighbor loses his job. Depression is when you lose yours.

—RONALD REAGAN

If you aren't fired up with enthusiasm, you will be fired with enthusiasm.

—VINCE LOMBARDI,
AMERICAN FOOTBALL COACH

When you first receive the news that you've been canned, it's common to try to determine where you went wrong. Was it your unkempt appearance, lack of motivation, or constant uncontrollable sobbing that did you in? Perhaps a combination of the three?

Regardless of what excuse your boss gives you, it stands to reason that you—like the following a**holes—did something to deserve your fate. Few bosses just throw darts at a board and fire whoever's name they hit—although that certainly does happen. Rather than try to make sense of the situation, perhaps it's best to just shrug it off and find a company that's unionized next time.

I used to be a window cleaner. I got fired because I sometimes liked to drink the soapy water.

—JAMELIA,
BRITISH SINGER AND MODEL

Most people treat the office manual the way they treat a software manual. They never look at it.

—JAMES LEVINE, AMERICAN
CONDUCTOR AND PIANIST

You moon the wrong person at an office party and suddenly you're not "professional" anymore.

—Jeff Foxworthy,
American comedian

A baseball game is

twice as much fun

if you're seeing it on

the company's time.

—William Feather,
American author

Researchers at Harvard say that taking a power nap for an hour in the afternoon can totally refresh you. They say that by the time you wake up, you'll feel so good, you'll be able to start looking for a new job.

—Jay Leno

You never ask why you've been fired because if you do, they're liable to tell you.

—Jerry Coleman,
baseball analyst

I went out there for a thousand a week, and I worked Monday, and I got fired Wednesday. The guy that hired me was out of town Tuesday.

—Nelson Algren,
American author

Sometimes I lie awake at night and ask, "Where have I gone wrong?" Then a voice says to me, "This is going to take more than one night."

—Charles Schulz, American
cartoonist and creator of
the "Peanuts" comics

No man goes before his time—unless the boss leaves early.

—Groucho Marx

It's hard to get fired from the government. You have to, like, kill people.

—Wanda Sykes,
American comedian

Thanks to a few forward-thinking a**holes, the United States has a safety net in place for delinquent employees. Those willing to swallow their pride can accept handouts from their fellow taxpayers in the form of unemployment insurance. Individuals used to have to endure public shamings and stand in line to receive their checks, but modern technology makes it possible to collect unemployment from the privacy of your own recliner. So the question now isn't "When are you going to find a new job?" It's "Why would you?"

Unemployment insurance is a prepaid vacation for freeloaders.

—RONALD REAGAN

Everybody was saying we must have more leisure. Now they are complaining they are unemployed.

—PRINCE PHILIP

I wish my brother would learn a trade so I would know what kind of work he's out of.

—HENNY YOUNGMAN,
BRITISH COMEDIAN

Now joblessness isn't just for philosophy majors.

—KENT BROCKMAN,
THE SIMPSONS

I'm a concert pianist. That's a pretentious way of saying "I'm unemployed at the moment."

—OSCAR LEVANT,
AMERICAN MUSICIAN AND ACTOR

The trouble with unemployment is that the minute you wake up in the morning, you're on the job.

—SLAPPY WHITE,
AMERICAN COMEDIAN AND ACTOR

Unemployment is like a headache or a high temperature—unpleasant and exhausting but not carrying in itself any explanation of its cause.

—WILLIAM HENRY BEVERIDGE,
BRITISH ECONOMIST

After the initial shock of losing your job sets in, it's time to take stock of the situation. You don't have to wake up early every morning. You don't have to deal with incompetent coworkers. And the only responsibility you have is calling the unemployment office once a week and remembering to feed yourself. Jackpot. Instead of cleaning up your desk with your head downcast in shame, you should run into your boss's office and give her a big old bear hug. She may have just done you the biggest favor of your life.

I have been with many men approaching death, and not one has ever said, "I only regret that I didn't spend more time at the office."

—DENNIS PRAGER,
CONSERVATIVE RADIO TALK
SHOW HOST

Handled creatively, getting fired allows an executive to actually experience a sense of relief that he never wanted the job he has lost.

—FRANK P. LOUCHHEIM,
AMERICAN BUSINESSMAN

It can be liberating to get fired because you realize the world doesn't end. There's other ways to make money, better jobs.

—RON LIVINGSTON,
AMERICAN ACTOR

Too much work and too much energy kill a man just as effectively as too much assorted vice or too much drink.

—RUDYARD KIPLING

It's just a job.

Grass grows, birds fly,

waves pound

the sand.

I beat people up.

—MUHAMMAD ALI

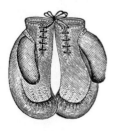

For a lot of people, getting fired means more than just losing a consistent source of income. It means losing all sense of identity. When asked, "What do you do?" they used to dive into a well-rehearsed self-promotional pitch about synergizing client bases. Now they just stare off into space and start breathing heavily. Fortunately there is hope for these pathetic individuals. If they can take a cue from some of these a**holes and embrace mediocrity, they can learn that it's okay to be unimpressive.

In order to go on living, one must try to escape the death involved in perfectionism.

—HANNAH ARENDT,
GERMAN POLITICAL THEORIST

Twenty years ago there was a stigma about being laid off; now it's the norm.

—MICHAEL WORTHINGTON,
CO-FOUNDER OF
RESUMEDOCTOR.COM

There's nothing wrong with being fired.

—TED TURNER,
AMERICAN BUSINESSMAN AND
FOUNDER OF TURNER
BROADCASTING SYSTEM, INC.

Accept that some days you are the pigeon, and some days you are the statue.

—DILBERT, *DILBERT*

I'm now as free as the breeze—with roughly the same income.

—GENE PERRET,
AMERICAN COMEDY WRITER

While a new job may be the last thing you want in your life right now, if you want to feed and clothe yourself going forward, you will probably need to get one. Depending on how long it's been since you applied for your last job, you may be in for a rude awakening. For one, jobs aren't exactly falling from the heavens like they were in years past. Also, that impressive philosophy BA you graduated with in 1992 is about as worthless now as the Pogs you bought that same year. But never fear: If you bone up on your ass-kissing abilities and review the following quotes, you should be fine.

Man is so made that he can only find relaxation from one kind of labor by taking up another.

—ANATOLE FRANCE, FRENCH POET

A lot of people quit looking for work as soon as they find a job.

—ZIG ZIGLAR, AMERICAN MOTIVATIONAL SPEAKER

I thought I wanted a career; turns out I just wanted a salary.

—UNKNOWN

I'd like to hire all American workers, but nobody will come to work for us knowing they'll be laid off in six or seven months.

—CHRIS HAYES, VICE PRESIDENT OF GROUNDMASTERS

They'll totally hire me if I say I got fired from my job on the Hill because of a sex scandal.

—JESSICA CUTLER, AMERICAN AUTHOR AND FORMER CONGRESSIONAL STAFF ASSISTANT

It's said in Hollywood that you should always forgive your enemies—because you never know when you'll have to work with them.

—LANA TURNER, AMERICAN ACTRESS

Sometimes in war, a preemptive strike is necessary to prevent future bloodshed. The same can be said for the workplace. When you get the sense that your boss is about to fire you, that might be a great time to consider quitting. Some might find the "I'm taking my ball and going home" approach a little childish, and they'd be right. But why give your boss the satisfaction of firing you when you can turn the tables and fire him?

The only liberty an inferior man really cherishes is the liberty to quit work, stretch out in the sun, and scratch himself.

—H. L. MENCKEN,
AMERICAN JOURNALIST

People ask what it takes to become a successful rock band. I always say just fucking quit your job and live on the street. And when you get really hungry, you'll come up with something good.

—PAUL LEARY, GUITARIST
FOR THE BUTTHOLE SURFERS

It is time I stepped aside for less experienced and less able men.

—SCOTT ELLADGE, AMERICAN
AUTHOR AND PROFESSOR ON HIS
RETIREMENT FROM CORNELL

I didn't quit movies. They quit me.

—JANE POWELL,
AMERICAN SINGER AND ACTRESS

I quit my job just to quit. I didn't quit my job to write fiction. I just didn't want to work anymore.

—DON DELILLO,
AMERICAN NOVELIST

All ballplayers should quit when it starts to feel as if all the baselines run uphill.

—BABE RUTH

If you keep your head down and don't piss off too many people, you may avoid getting fired long enough to make it to the promised land: retirement. Say goodbye to stale coffee and lunch meetings, and hello to early-bird specials and daytime television. It may be sad that your single greatest accomplishment in life was not getting fired, but at least you never had to stand in line at the unemployment office.

When a man retires,

his wife gets twice

the husband but only

half the income.

—CHI CHI RODRIGUEZ, PUERTO RICAN PROFESSIONAL GOLFER

Retirement is wonderful. It's doing nothing without worrying about getting caught at it.

—GENE PERRET, AMERICAN COMEDY WRITER

Retirement at sixty-five is ridiculous. When I was sixty-five, I still had pimples.

—GEORGE BURNS, AMERICAN COMEDIAN AND ACTOR

The company accountant is shy and retiring. He's shy a quarter of a million dollars. That's why he's retiring.

—MILTON BERLE, AMERICAN COMEDIAN AND ACTOR

If you have a job without any aggravations, you don't have a job.

—MALCOLM S. FORBES, AMERICAN PUBLISHER

Retirement is like a long vacation in Las Vegas. The goal is to enjoy it the fullest, but not so fully that you run out of money.

—JONATHAN CLEMENTS, BRITISH AUTHOR

CHAPTER 11

MONEY

When it isn't busy being the root of all evil, money has a lot of practical applications in modern society. Aside from the obvious fact that it can be exchanged for goods and services, money can also get you laid, help you make friends, increase your self-esteem, and even replicate itself when handled properly. So why then is it the single most vilified inanimate object in history?

There are numerous theories as to why people hate money so much, but most of them are lengthy, complicated, and ultimately wrong. The truth is that people don't hate money at all. They just hate the a**holes who have so much of it. And who could blame them? It's easy to get pissy when you make $7.50 an hour sorting through garbage while a Wall Street executive makes 100 times that amount taking a shit. But whether your bank account is spilling off the page or your life savings fits inside a coffee can, you can learn a thing or two about money from the following a**holes, both rich and poor.

Come away! Poverty's catching.

—Aphra Behn, British writer

If it's a good script, I'll do it. If it's a bad script, and they pay me enough, I'll do it.

—George Burns,
American comedian and actor

A successful man is one who makes more money than his wife can spend. A successful woman is one who can find such a man.

—Lana Turner,
American actress

Every morning, I get up and look through the Forbes list of the richest people in America. If I'm not there, I go to work.

—Robert Orben, American
magician and writer

You can be young without money, but you can't be old without it.

—Tennessee Williams,
American playwright
and author

That's the thing about Mother Nature: She really doesn't care what economic bracket you're in.

—Whoopi Goldberg

Bills travel through the mail at twice the speed of checks.

—J. Steven Wright,
American comedian

If you can count your money, you don't have a billion dollars.

—Paul Getty,
American businessman

We were never aware of our financial situation.

—Ashley Olsen,
American actress

The only way not to think about money is to have a great deal of it.

—EDITH WHARTON,
AMERICAN NOVELIST

When a man tells you that he got rich through hard work, ask him: "Whose?"

—DON MARQUIS,
AMERICAN JOURNALIST

A rich man's joke is always funny.

—THOMAS BROWNE,
BRITISH AUTHOR

I know of nothing more despicable and pathetic than a man who devotes all of the hours of the waking day to the making of money for money's sake.

—JOHN D. ROCKEFELLER

Bart, with $10,000, we'd be millionaires! We could buy all kinds of useful things like . . . love!

—HOMER J. SIMPSON,
THE SIMPSONS

Someday I want to be rich. Some people get so rich they lose all respect for humanity. That's how rich I want to be.

—RITA RUDNER, AMERICAN
ACTRESS AND COMEDIAN

If you think money has no hold over you, I regret to inform you that you are sorely mistaken. Need proof? If you spot a $20 bill laying on the ground, do you get excited and pick it up? 'Nuff said.

But you shouldn't feel bad about money's stranglehold over your psyche. As the following quotes show, money is the be all and end all of human civilization. If you were equally obsessed with worthless things like love, friendship, and good health, then you might be in trouble.

Wine maketh merry: but money answereth all things.

—BIBLE, ECCLESIASTES, 10:19

Money won't buy happiness, but it will pay the salaries of a large research staff to study the problem.

—WILLIAM E. "BILL" VAUGHAN,
AMERICAN COLUMNIST

Whenever people say, "We mustn't be sentimental," you can take it they are about to do something cruel. And if they add, "We must be realistic," they mean they are going to make money out of it.

—BRIGID BROPHY,
BRITISH NOVELIST

There's a phrase we live by in America: "In God We Trust." It's right there where Jesus would want it: on our money.

—STEPHEN COLBERT,
AMERICAN POLITICAL SATIRIST

Money can't buy you happiness, but it does bring you a more pleasant form of misery.

—SPIKE MILLIGAN,
IRISH COMEDIAN

What's the use of
happiness? It can't
buy you money.

—HENNY YOUNGMAN,
BRITISH COMEDIAN

A large income is the best recipe for happiness I ever heard of.

—JANE AUSTEN

Despite all the evidence to the contrary, there are some individuals who are not convinced that money is really all that great. True, most of these people are poor and don't know what they are talking about, but there are a few wealthy people who feel this way as well. While there's not much to say to the destitute members of the I Hate Money Club, the rich a**holes in this camp should stop bitching. After all, there are plenty of people out there who will do everything in their power to relieve them of their terrible burden.

Thinking to get at once all the gold the goose could give, he killed it and opened it only to find—nothing.

—AESOP

If you want to know what God thinks of money, just look at the people he gave it to.

—DOROTHY PARKER,
AMERICAN POET

Most of the rich people I've known have been fairly miserable.

—AGATHA CHRISTIE

A moderate addiction to money may not always be hurtful, but when taken in excess, it is nearly always bad for the health.

—CLARENCE DAY,
AMERICAN AUTHOR

Make money your god and it will plague you like the devil.

—HENRY FIELDING,
BRITISH NOVELIST

A business that makes nothing but money is a poor business.

—HENRY FORD

Before borrowing money from a friend, decide which you need most.

—PROVERB

All progress is based upon a universal innate desire on the part of every organism to live beyond its income.

—SAMUEL BUTLER,
VICTORIAN NOVELIST

While it's true that money can't buy you happiness, poverty sure as hell can't either. And there is no better reminder of how important money can be than not having any at all. But before you complain about how broke you are, just remember you are in much better shape than some of the following a**holes.

If you ever have to steal money from your kid, and later on he discovers it's gone, I think a good thing to do is to blame it on Santa Claus.

—JACK HANDEY,
AMERICAN COMEDIAN

You don't seem to realize that a poor person who is unhappy is in a better position than a rich person who is unhappy. Because the poor person has hope. He thinks money would help.

—JEAN KERR, AMERICAN
AUTHOR AND PLAYWRIGHT

I used to think I was poor. Then they told me I wasn't poor, I was needy. Then they told me it was self-defeating to think of myself as needy. I was deprived. (Oh not deprived but rather underprivileged.) Then they told me that underprivileged was overused. I was disadvantaged. I still don't have a dime. But I have a great vocabulary.

—JULES FEIFFER, CREATOR OF
THE COMIC STRIP *FEIFFER*

I used to sell furniture for a living. The trouble was, it was my own.

—LES DAWSON,
BRITISH COMEDIAN

The lack of money is the root of all evil.

—MARK TWAIN

They say it is better to be poor and happy than rich and miserable, but how about a compromise like moderately rich and just moody?

—PRINCESS DIANA

The easiest way for your children to learn about money is for you not to have any.

—KATHARINE WHITEHORN,
BRITISH COLUMNIST

A fool and his money are soon parted.

—PROVERB

When shit becomes valuable, the poor will be born without a**holes.

—HENRY MILLER, AMERICAN NOVELIST

Another good thing about being poor is that when you are seventy, your children will not have declared you legally insane in order to gain control of your estate.

—WOODY ALLEN

For those without the skills or breeding necessary to earn huge wads of cash themselves, there is another means to obtain an unexpected windfall: charity. True, you generally need to be going through some pretty hard times to cash in, but sometimes you need to weigh your options.

One of the serious obstacles to the improvement of our race is indiscriminate charity.

—ANDREW CARNEGIE, SCOTTISH BUSINESSMAN AND FOUNDER OF THE CARNEGIE STEEL COMPANY

Money is like manure: of very little use except it be spread.

—FRANCIS BACON, BRITISH PHILOSOPHER

A man receiving charity always hates his benefactor—it is a fixed characteristic of human nature.

—GEORGE ORWELL, BRITISH AUTHOR AND JOURNALIST

Charity degrades those who receive it and hardens those who dispense it.

—GEORGE SAND, FRENCH NOVELIST

Charity is injurious unless it helps the recipient to become independent of it.

—JOHN D. ROCKEFELLER

No one would remember the Good Samaritan if he'd only had good intentions. He had money as well.

—MARGARET THATCHER

It is justice, not charity, that is wanting in the world.

—MARY SHELLEY,
BRITISH NOVELIST

Never stand begging for what you have the power to earn.

—MIGUEL DE CERVANTES
SAAVEDRA, SPANISH NOVELIST

Lots of people think they're charitable if they give away their old clothes and things they don't want.

—MYRTLE REED,
AMERICAN AUTHOR

The worst of charity is that the lives you are asked to preserve are not worth preserving.

—RALPH WALDO EMERSON

A charitable man is like an apple tree—he gives his fruit and is silent; the philanthropist is like the hen.

—UNKNOWN

Few can explain the concept of credit better than Popeye's fiscally irresponsible friend Wimpy, who famously remarked, "I'll gladly pay you Tuesday for a hamburger today." Replace "Tuesday" with "never" and "hamburger" with "everything," and you basically have the mindset of the American public. After all, it's not that we can't live within our means, we'd just rather live within somebody else's.

It is only the poor who pay cash, and that not from virtue, but because they are refused credit.

—ANATOLE FRANCE,
FRENCH POET

Neither a borrower or a lender be/For Loan oft loses both itself and friend.

—WILLIAM SHAKESPEARE

Credit is a system whereby a person who cannot pay gets another person who cannot pay to guarantee that he can pay.

—CHARLES DICKENS

If you think nobody cares if you're alive, try missing a couple of car payments.

—EARL WILSON,
AMERICAN COLUMNIST

Modern man drives a mortgaged car over a bond-financed highway on credit-card gas.

—EARL WILSON,
AMERICAN COLUMNIST

A banker is a fellow who lends you his umbrella when the sun is shining and wants it back the minute it begins to rain.

—MARK TWAIN

It is a little known fact that money, when buried in the dark recesses of a bank vault, can slowly grow and result in more money. Scientists are unsure whether this reproduction is sexual or asexual, but the end result is the same. Unfortunately, this process requires that the owner of said money refrain from spending any of it during this time. Because of this regrettable fact, the vast majority of people miss out on this inconvenient but lucrative opportunity.

The surest way to establish your credit is to work yourself into the position of not needing any.

—MAURICE SWITZER,
AMERICAN AUTHOR

A nickel ain't worth

a dime anymore.

—YOGI BERRA,
AMERICAN BASEBALL MANAGER
AND FORMER PLAYER

When your bank account is so overdrawn that it is positively photographic, steps must be taken.

—DOROTHY PARKER,
AMERICAN POET

I've got all the money I'll ever need, if I die by four o'clock.

—HENNY YOUNGMAN,
BRITISH COMEDIAN

A bank is a place that will lend you money if you can prove that you don't need it.

—BOB HOPE

You see those charts that say if you put away $500 a year starting at age 20, by the time you're 50, you'd have a gazillion dollars? It just makes you ill that you didn't do it.

—JAMES CARVILLE, AMERICAN
POLITICAL COMMENTATOR

When we don't keep good track of it, money has a tendency to wander off and find its way into strange places. Like jewelry counters, liquor stores, and strip clubs. This is why it is very important to develop a foolproof accounting scheme to make sure it stays where it's supposed to. This can range from detailed spreadsheets and graphs to less sophisticated scribblings on cocktail napkins— as long as some effort is made to keep track.

Keeping accounts, sir, is of no use when a man is spending his own money and has nobody to whom he is to account. You won't eat less beef today, because you have written down what it cost yesterday.

—SAMUEL JOHNSON,
BRITISH AUTHOR

We can tell our values by looking at our checkbook stubs.

—GLORIA STEINEM,
AMERICAN FEMINIST

April is tax month. If you are having trouble filing your taxes, then you should hire an accountant. They'll give you the same advice that they've given hundreds of corporations—taxes are for douche bags.

—ED HELMS, AMERICAN ACTOR

I'm kidding about having only a few dollars. I might have a few dollars more.

—JAMES BROWN

Bankruptcy is a legal proceeding in which you put your money in your pants pocket and give your coat to your creditors.

—JOEY ADAMS,
AMERICAN COMEDIAN

I'm a writer. I write checks. They're not very good.

—WENDY LIEBMAN,
AMERICAN COMEDIAN

CHAPTER 12

POWER

No other intangible entity possesses the transformative ability that power enjoys. You could be the most nerdy, meek individual on the planet, but as soon as somebody gives you a badge and a uniform, you become a raging torrent of a**holeness hell-bent on imposing your will on anyone in a ten-mile radius. But the truly amazing thing is not that you've changed; it's that people actually start to listen to you.

Because it is so volatile, power is generally reserved for people who know what they are doing with it. But every now and then, some undeserving douche bag manages to wrestle some away for himself or herself. But rest assured, when that happens, there are always a wealth of a**holes available to express their displeasure.

To limit the press is to insult a nation; to prohibit reading of certain books is to declare the inhabitants to be either fools or slaves.

—CLAUDE ADRIEN HELVÉTIUS,
FRENCH PHILOSOPHER

Never underestimate the power of the State to act out its own massive fantasies.

—DON DELILLO,
AMERICAN NOVELIST

I know of nothing sublime which is not some modification of power.

—EDMUND BURKE, BRITISH
STATESMAN AND PHILOSOPHER

Power is not something that can be assumed or discarded at will like underwear.

—JOHN KENNETH GALBRAITH,
CANADIAN-AMERICAN ECONOMIST

Those who seek power are not worthy of that power.

—PLATO

Too bad all the people who know how to run the country are busy driving taxicabs and cutting hair.

—GEORGE BURNS,
AMERICAN COMEDIAN AND ACTOR

The only real power comes out of a long rifle.

—JOSEPH STALIN

Even one billion Chinese do not a superpower make.

—JOHN LUKACS,
AMERICAN HISTORIAN

If you have selfish, ignorant citizens, you're going to get selfish, ignorant leaders.

—GEORGE CARLIN,
AMERICAN COMEDIAN

What do all men with power want? More power.

—THE ORACLE,
THE MATRIX RELOADED

When humans gain any sort of power, there is a natural inclination to hold on to it for dear life. It is a rare instance indeed when somebody in power will simply roll over and give it up. More often than not, power has to be taken with force. While this fact clearly applies to power-hungry dictators and CEOs, it even extends all the way down to lowly hall monitors or that creepy guy who organizes your neighborhood watch program. Depending on the circumstances, the techniques used to usurp power will be different, but the principle is the same: strike hard and strike fast.

What most people don't seem to realize is that there is just as much money to be made out of the wreckage of a civilization as from the upbuilding of one.

—RHETT BUTLER,
GONE WITH THE WIND

You can get much farther with a kind word and a gun than you can with a kind word alone.

—AL CAPONE

I have heard there are troubles of more than one kind. Some come from ahead, and some come from behind. But I've bought a big bat. I'm all ready, you see. Now my troubles are going to have troubles with me!

—DR. SEUSS

Political power grows out of the barrel of a gun.

—MAO TSE-TUNG,
CHINESE REVOLUTIONARY AND
FOUNDER OF THE PEOPLE'S
REPUBLIC OF CHINA

I like power and I like to use it.

—SAM RAYBURN,
FORMER SPEAKER OF THE U.S.
HOUSE OF REPRESENTATIVES

What do I care about law? Ain't I got the power?

—CORNELIUS VANDERBILT,
AMERICAN BUSINESSMAN

Diplomacy is the art of saying "Nice doggie" until you can find a rock.

—WILL ROGERS,
AMERICAN COMEDIAN AND ACTOR

The dumber people think you are, the more surprised they're going to be when you kill them.

—WILLIAM CLAYTON,
MORMON MINISTER

Why don't you bring your face up here and let me punch it? Then you can tell me (if I'm stronger).

—SHAQUILLE O'NEAL,
AMERICAN BASKETBALL PLAYER

Probably the easiest method for obtaining power is to rise up on the shoulders of those weaker than you. Not only is stepping on the little guy a time-honored tradition, it's also far safer than taking on the big guy. While there is a remote possibility that the little guys will resist your attempts, chances are, they will simply curl up into a ball and wait for the danger to pass.

When I was a kid, I used to pray every night for a new bicycle. Then I realized that the Lord doesn't work that way, so I stole one and asked Him to forgive me.

—EMO PHILIPS,
AMERICAN COMEDIAN

Our sense of power is more vivid when we break a man's spirit than when we win his heart.

—ERIC HOFFER,
AMERICAN PHILOSOPHER

If you've got them by the balls, their hearts and minds will follow.

—JOHN WAYNE

The secret of power is the knowledge that others are more cowardly than you are.

—KARL LUDWIG BÖRNE,
GERMAN POLITICAL WRITER

If you pick up a starving dog and make him prosperous, he will not bite you. This is the principal difference between a dog and a man.

—MARK TWAIN

Power without abuse loses its charm.

—PAUL VALÉRY, FRENCH POET

Kill one man, and you are a murderer. Kill millions of men, and you are a conqueror. Kill them all, and you are a god.

—JEAN ROSTAND, FRENCH
BIOLOGIST AND PHILOSOPHER

For the most part, there are absolutely no drawbacks to limitless power. You can do whatever you want, everybody pretends to love you, and you get to see movies before they come out in theaters. That being said, there will always be the occasional killjoy around to rain on your parade. Some will suggest you stop using your position for personal gain, or that maybe your power is going to your head. Silly things like that. You can certainly dismiss them if you'd like (or have them killed), but some of these a**holes do seem to know what they are talking about.

The attempt to combine wisdom and power has only rarely been successful and then only for a short while.

—ALBERT EINSTEIN

It is said that power corrupts, but actually it's more true that power attracts the corruptible. The sane are usually attracted by other things than power.

—DAVID BRIN, AMERICAN
SCIENCE FICTION WRITER

You can't trust anybody with power.

—Newt Gingrich, former Speaker of the U.S. House of Representatives

During the whole period of written history, it is not the workers but the robbers who have been in control of the world.

—Scott Nearing, American conservationist

In the past, those who foolishly sought power by riding on the back of the tiger ended up inside.

—John F. Kennedy

Power corrupts and absolute power corrupts absolutely.

—Lord Acton, letter to Bishop Mandell Creighton, 1887

A friend in power is a friend lost.

—Henry Adams, American journalist and grandson to John Quincy Adams

Once you have conquered all there is to conquer, acquired all there is to acquire, and stepped on everyone there is to step on, it's time to reflect on your epic rise to power. The first thing you may notice is, since you've screwed over all your friends to get there, it's rather lonely at the top. The second is that a crowd of angry, disenfranchised subjects are gathering at the bottom getting ready to stage a revolt. The third thing you may notice is that being powerful might not be everything it's cracked up to be. Had you listened to the advice of the following a**holes, you might have realized this sooner.

In life there are no winners, only a**holes with Swiss bank accounts.

—Matthew Lotti, American author

If I had known what it would be like to have it all—I might have been willing to settle for less.

—LILY TOMLIN

Success didn't spoil me; I've always been insufferable.

—FRAN LEBOWITZ,
AMERICAN AUTHOR

You can't have everything . . . where would you put it?

—STEVEN WRIGHT,
AMERICAN COMEDIAN

Nearly all men can stand adversity, but if you want to test a man's character, give him power.

—ABRAHAM LINCOLN

The only thing more gratifying than watching someone gradually rise to a position of power is to witness their swift and inevitable fall from grace. Call it jealousy, call it envy, call it whatever you'd like, but there's no denying how strangely satisfying it is to witness a failure that isn't your own—for a change. This explains why everyone always knows what should have been done differently, but nobody ever has the foresight to speak up ahead of time—except for the few assorted a**holes you'll find here.

America will never be destroyed from the outside. If we falter and lose our freedoms, it will be because we destroyed ourselves.

—ABRAHAM LINCOLN

Arbitrary power is like most other things which are very hard, very liable to be broken.

—ABIGAIL ADAMS

The most common way people give up their power is by thinking they don't have any.

—ALICE WALKER,
AMERICAN AUTHOR

Power does not cor-

rupt. Fear corrupts

. . . perhaps the fear

of a loss of power.

—JOHN STEINBECK

Better to be king for a night, than a schmuck for a lifetime.

—RUPERT PUPKIN,
THE KING OF COMEDY

Their insatiable lust for power is only equaled by their incurable impotence in exercising it.

—WINSTON CHURCHILL

Anyone who has ever torched a colony of ants with a magnifying glass knows firsthand the appeal of complete and ultimate power. As far as your miniature subjects are concerned, you are a living god exacting judgment on their miserable souls. While things get a little trickier when you upgrade from ants to humans, the general principles are the same. Just upgrade your magnifying glass to tomahawk missiles and the threat of nuclear proliferation and you should be all set.

All I want is a warm bed and a kind word and unlimited power.

—ASHLEIGH BRILLIANT,
AMERICAN CARTOONIST

I shall be an autocrat, that's my trade; and the good Lord will forgive me, that's his.

—CATHERINE THE GREAT

Those in possession of absolute power can not only prophesy and make their prophecies come true, but they can also lie and make their lies come true.

—ERIC HOFFER,
AMERICAN PHILOSOPHER

Power is the ultimate aphrodisiac.

—Henry Kissinger,
American diplomat

Power is when you have every justification to kill someone, and then you don't.

—Oskar Schindler,
German industrialist and
inspiration for the novel
Schindler's Ark, and the
film Schindler's List

Adversity makes men, and prosperity makes monsters.

—Victor Hugo,
French poet and author

The superpowers often behave like two heavily armed blind men feeling their way around a room, each believing himself in mortal peril from the other, whom he assumes to have perfect vision.

—Henry Kissinger,
American diplomat

While it's true you can be powerful by blowing things up and ruling with an iron fist, there are also more subtle ways to influence people. With one magic word, a common individual can be just as powerful as any president or king. And that word is success.

Successful people like actors, CEOs, and low-level politicians have enough money and clout to impose their will on the masses without anyone even noticing they are doing so. Fortunately for the rest of us, most of them are far too busy wallowing in their own self-righteousness to think of using their powers for evil.

The worst part of success is to try to find someone who is happy for you.

—Bette Midler

Success is often the result of taking a misstep in the right direction.

—AL BERNSTEIN,
AMERICAN SPORTSCASTER

The Lord gave us two ends—one to sit on and the other to think with. Success depends on which one we use the most.

—ANN LANDERS

Success to me is having ten honeydew melons and eating only the top half of each one.

—BARBRA STREISAND

If hard work is the

key to success, most

people would rather

pick the lock.

—CLAUDE MCDONALD,
BRITISH DIPLOMAT

A successful man is one who can lay a firm foundation with the bricks others have thrown at him.

—DAVID BRINKLEY,
AMERICAN NEWSCASTER

Success is simply a matter of luck. Ask any failure.

—EARL WILSON,
AMERICAN COLUMNIST

Don't confuse fame with success. Madonna is one; Helen Keller is the other.

—ERMA BOMBECK,
AMERICAN HUMORIST

All you need in this life is ignorance and confidence, and then success is sure.

—MARK TWAIN

My formula
for success
is rise early,
work late, and
strike oil.

—J. PAUL GETTY,
AMERICAN BUSINESSMAN

For the majority of recorded history, power was a luxury reserved exclusively for men. And if you take the time to read that recorded history, you will quickly discover that may not have been such a good idea.

It's impossible to know if historical events like the crucifixion of Jesus, the Crusades, World War II, and September 11th would have had better outcomes had women been ruling the world. But it's difficult to imagine they could have ended much worse.

Being powerful is like being a lady. If you have to tell people you are, you aren't.

—MARGARET THATCHER

Proof that they do not understand the republic is that in their fine promises for universal suffrage, they forgot women.

—DELPHINE DE GIRARDIN,
FRENCH AUTHOR

We've always been ready for female superheroes. Because women want to be them and men want to do them.

—FAMKE JANSSEN,
DUTCH ACTRESS

Men should think
twice before making
widowhood women's
only path to power.

—GLORIA STEINEM,
AMERICAN FEMINIST

The truth is that all men having power ought to be mistrusted.

—JAMES MADISON

Always remember the first rule of power tactics: Power is not only what you have but what the enemy thinks you have.

—SAUL ALINSKY,
AMERICAN COMMUNITY
ORGANIZER AND WRITER

When women are depressed, they eat or go shopping. Men invade another country. It's a whole different way of thinking.

—ELAYNE BOOSLER, AMERICAN
ACTRESS AND COMEDIAN

PART 4

KICK-ASS COMPETITIONS

People understand contests. You take a bunch of kids throwing rocks at random and people look askance, but if you go and hold a rock-throwing contest—people understand that.

—Don Murray, Scottish footballer

CHAPTER 13

SPORTS

For humans with exceptional speed, stamina, strength, coordination, and focus, sporting events offer an opportunity to achieve immortality. For everyone else, it's an excuse to wear face paint, scream like an idiot, and drink overpriced beer out of plastic cups. Everybody wins.

Our fascination with sports begins at an early age. Depending on our body type and skill level, we gravitate toward fast-paced games like kickball (tall, lean children) or more modest contests like Pokémon (slow, overweight kids). This trend continues until the former grow up to be superstar athletes and the latter turn into the belligerent, drunken fans that cheer for them.

Despite their drastically different roles, both players and fans possess a single shared belief: Sports are the single most important thing in the known universe. Because there are so many different sporting events occurring at any given time, sports are unique in that they can simultaneously be equally important.

While no one is quite certain why humans feel the need to participate in such barbaric competitions, many of history's greatest a**holes have lent their opinion on the matter.

Watching football is like watching pornography. There's plenty of action, and I can't take my eyes off it, but when it's over, I wonder why the hell I spent an afternoon doing it.

—LUKE SALISBURY,
AMERICAN AUTHOR

Ability is the art of getting credit for all the home runs somebody else hits.

—CASEY STENGEL,
MLB OUTFIELDER

When it comes to sports, I am not particularly interested. Generally speaking, I look upon them as dangerous and tiring activities performed by people with whom I share nothing except the right to trial by jury.

—FRAN LEBOWITZ,
AMERICAN AUTHOR

October is not only a beautiful month but marks the precious yet fleeting overlap of hockey, baseball, basketball, and football.

—JASON LOVE,
AMERICAN COMEDIAN

I asked a ref if he could give me a technical foul for thinking bad things about him. He said, "Of course not." I said, "Well, I think you stink." And he gave me a technical. You can't trust 'em.

—JIM VALVANO, COACH OF THE
1983 NORTH CAROLINA UNIVER-
SITY MEN'S BASKETBALL TEAM

Ninety percent of the game is half mental.

—JIM WOHFORD, AMERICAN
MAJOR LEAGUE OUTFIELDER

The ball is man's most disastrous invention, not excluding the wheel.

—ROBERT MORLEY,
BRITISH ACTOR

The only winning move is not to play.

—WOPR (WAR OPERATION PLAN RESPONSE), *WARGAMES*

Men do not quit playing because they grow old; they grow old because they quit playing.

—OLIVER WENDELL HOLMES, AMERICAN WRITER

In America, the more likely a participant is to be fatally injured during a sporting event, the more popular it is. This explains why cricket, the only sporting event that breaks for tea, has yet to gain an American audience. It's not that we enjoy watching people get hurt. It's just that we don't enjoy watching people *not* get hurt, which is a subtle but important distinction to make. Sure, there is certainly room for sports with less physical contact in American culture, but the only ones worth discussing involve at least a little blood.

There are several differences between a football game and a revolution. For one thing, a football game usually lasts longer and the participants wear uniforms. Also, there are usually more casualties in a football game. The object of the game is to move a ball past the other team's goal line. This counts as six points. No points are given for lacerations, contusions, or abrasions, but then no points are deducted either. Kicking is very important in football. In fact, some of the more enthusiastic players even kick the ball, occasionally.

—ALFRED HITCHCOCK

Some people think football is a matter of life and death. I don't like that attitude. I can assure them it is much more serious than that.

—BILL SHANKLY, BRITISH SOCCER COACH

Sharks are as tough as those football fans who take their shirts off during games in Chicago in January, only more intelligent.

—DAVE BARRY, AMERICAN AUTHOR AND COLUMNIST

There's more to boxing than hitting. There's not getting hit, for instance.

—GEORGE FOREMAN,
AMERICAN BOXER

Baseball, it is said, is only a game. True. And the Grand Canyon is only a hole in Arizona. Not all holes, or games, are created equal.

—GEORGE WILL,
AMERICAN JOURNALIST

Football combines the two worst features of America life: It is violence punctuated by committee meetings.

—GEORGE WILL,
AMERICAN JOURNALIST

Rugby is a beastly game played by gentlemen. Soccer is a gentleman's game played by beasts. Football is a beastly game played by beasts.

—HENRY BLAHA,
AMERICAN FOOTBALL PLAYER

Football is, after all, a wonderful way to get rid of your aggressions without going to jail for it.

—HEYWOOD HALE BROUN,
AMERICAN JOURNALIST

Football is all very well a good game for rough girls, but not for delicate boys.

—OSCAR WILDE

The NFL, like life, is full of idiots.

—RANDY CROSS, FORMER
NFL OFFENSIVE LINEMAN

While all the real athletes were off beating each other to a bloody pulp, a few genetically inferior a**holes thought it might be fun to make up their own sports. Ones better suited to nonathletic types like themselves. Thus sports like darts, fishing, golf, and archery were born. It's not that such competitions don't require skill. They most certainly do. But it's difficult to call yourself an athlete when the most taxing movement you perform is applying chalk to a wooden stick.

Fishing is boring, unless you catch an actual fish, and then it is disgusting.

—DAVE BARRY, AMERICAN
AUTHOR AND COLUMNIST

Golf is played by 20 million mature American men whose wives think they are out having fun.

—JIM BISHOP,
AMERICAN JOURNALIST

Golf is a good walk spoiled.

—MARK TWAIN

The depressing thing about tennis is that no matter how good I get, I'll never be as good as a wall.

—MITCH HEDBERG,
AMERICAN COMEDIAN

There's a fine line between fishing and just standing on the shore like an idiot.

—STEVEN WRIGHT,
AMERICAN COMEDIAN

Playing polo is like trying to play golf during an earthquake.

—SYLVESTER STALLONE,
AMERICAN ACTOR

Skiing combines outdoor fun with knocking down trees with your face.

—DAVE BARRY, AMERICAN
AUTHOR AND COLUMNIST

Golf is a game whose aim is to hit a very small ball into an even smaller hole, with weapons singularly ill-designed for the purpose.

—WINSTON CHURCHILL

It may be that all games are silly. But then, so are humans.

—ROBERT LYND,
IRISH JOURNALIST

I don't think the discus will ever attract any interest until they let us start throwing them at one another.

—AL OERTER,
OLYMPIC DISCUS CHAMPION

There is only one group of people who truly believe winning doesn't matter: losers. For everyone else, victory is more important than breathing. It's why they wake up in the morning, and it's the only reason they step onto the field. Winning is so important that they are willing to lie, cheat, and steal in order to do it. And if they can't win, then the game was stupid and they didn't want to play anyway.

Whoever is winning at the moment will always seem to be invincible.

—GEORGE ORWELL, BRITISH
AUTHOR AND JOURNALIST

Anybody can win, unless there happens to be a second entry.

—GEORGE BERNARD SHAW,
IRISH PLAYWRIGHT AND AUTHOR

I'm bi-winning. I win here, and I win there. Now what?

—CHARLIE SHEEN

If you make every game a life-and-death thing, you're going to have problems. You'll be dead a lot.

—DEAN SMITH,
FORMER COACH OF THE NORTH
CAROLINA UNIVERSITY MEN'S
BASKETBALL TEAM

Money was never a big motivation for me, except as a way to keep score. The real excitement is playing the game.

—DONALD TRUMP

If I were playing third base and my mother were rounding third with the run that was going to beat us, I'd trip her. Oh, I'd pick her up and brush her off and say, "Sorry, Mom, but nobody beats me."

—LEO DUROCHER, FORMER
MAJOR LEAGUE INFIELDER

People will often tell you there are worse things in life than losing, but these people are clearly losers. You'll be able to tell them apart from their more successful counterparts because losing leaves the afflicted a depressed, empty, bitter shell. The next time you want to console a group of losers, perhaps you should offer to put them out of their misery instead. That should cheer them up.

Finish last in your league and they call you Idiot. Finish last in medical school and they call you Doctor.

—ABE LEMONS, FORMER
OKLAHOMA CITY UNIVERSITY
MEN'S BASKETBALL COACH

I would have thought that the knowledge that you are going to be leapt upon by half-a-dozen congratulatory but sweaty teammates would be inducement not to score a goal.

—ARTHUR MARSHALL,
AMERICAN FOOTBALL PLAYER

If a tie is like kissing your sister, losing is like kissing your grandmother with her teeth out.

—GEORGE BRETT,
HALL OF FAME THIRD BASEMAN

A winner rebukes and forgives; a loser is too timid to rebuke and too petty to forgive.

—SYDNEY J. HARRIS,
AMERICAN JOURNALIST

Show me a good loser and I'll show you an idiot.

—LEO DUROCHER,
FORMER MAJOR LEAGUE
INFIELDER

I have not failed. I've just found 10,000 ways that won't work.

—THOMAS EDISON

We didn't lose the game; we just ran out of time.

—VINCE LOMBARDI,
AMERICAN FOOTBALL COACH

In typical conversation, there exists a laundry list of words humanity has decided simply shouldn't be said. There is one exception to this rule, and that is sports. During a sporting event, players and fans are free to say anything and everything they want to one another. There is no word too filthy nor insult too vile if it helps the speaker cope with the actions taking place in the game. True, this manner of cavalier speaking can result in the occasional drunken brawl, but for many people that is the only reason to attend a sporting event in the first place.

He's nice to people 'n' animals . . . but you oughta hear him talkin' to a golf ball!

—DENNIS THE MENACE,
DENNIS THE MENACE

'Twas but my tongue, 'twas not my soul that swore.

—EURIPIDES

Many a man's profanity has saved him from a nervous breakdown.

—Henry S. Haskins,
American writer

If profanity had an influence on the flight of the ball, the game of golf would be played far better than it is.

—Horace G. Hutchinson,
American golfer and author

I personally think we developed language because of our deep inner need to complain.

—Jane Wagner,
American writer

Under certain circumstances, urgent circumstances, desperate circumstances, profanity provides a relief denied even to prayer.

—Mark Twain

Swearing was invented as a compromise between running away and fighting.

—Finley Peter Dunne,
American humorist

Athletes are many things—strong, fast, coordinated, wealthy—but one thing they rarely are is smart. They are great when it comes to kicking and throwing, but strategy often escapes them. Enter the coach: a fast-talking, wise-cracking, has-been who can mold a motley crew of misfits into a winning team—provided he doesn't get fired first.

The fewer rules a coach has, the fewer rules there are for players to break.

—John Madden,
former American football
player and coach

If you don't win, you're going to be fired. If you do win, you've only put off the day you're going to be fired.

—LEO DUROCHER,
FORMER MAJOR LEAGUE
INFIELDER

Coaching is nothing more than eliminating mistakes before you get fired.

—LOU HOLTZ, FORMER
COLLEGE FOOTBALL COACH

We can't win at home and we can't win on the road. My problem as general manager is I can't think of another place to play.

—PAT WILLIAMS,
SENIOR VICE PRESIDENT OF THE
ORLANDO MAGIC

One day of practice is like one day of clean living. It doesn't do you any good.

—ABE LEMONS, FORMER
OKLAHOMA CITY UNIVERSITY
MEN'S BASKETBALL COACH

In sports, the secret to success lies in a combination of natural ability, intense training, and strong mental focus. But for the less talented, lazier athletes of the world, there is always the option to cheat. Similar to lying, cheating is only dangerous when the participants can't convince themselves they are doing something wrong. Because if the goal is to win, and you do so, then how can anything you do be considered cheating?

If you know how to cheat, start now.

—EARL WEAVER, BALTIMORE
ORIOLES GENERAL MANAGER

The sure way to be cheated is to think one's self more cunning than others.

—FRANÇOIS DE LA
ROCHEFOUCAULD,
FRENCH AUTHOR

Gimme: An agreement between two losers who can't putt.

—JIM BISHOP,
AMERICAN JOURNALIST

Old age and treachery will overcome youth and skill.

—PROVERB

No, we don't cheat. And even if we did, I'd never tell you.

—TOMMY LASORDA,
AMERICAN MAJOR LEAGUE
BASEBALL PLAYER AND
MANAGER

In order to preserve your self-respect, it is sometimes necessary to lie and cheat.

—ROBERT BYRNE,
AMERICAN PROFESSIONAL POOL
PLAYER AND AUTHOR

CHAPTER 14

WAR

While some arguments can by settled by a simple game of roshambo, there are some disputes that simply cannot be settled diplomatically. Luckily for humanity, we have yet to encounter a problem that cannot be solved by a good old-fashioned war. And if we ever do, we'll just blow it up anyway.

The time-honored tradition of warfare stems from our ancient ancestors. Noticing that their neighbors possessed an excess of food, they sought to liberate them of this unnecessary burden. Since their neighbors were quite unwilling to part with it, they then liberated them of their unnecessary heads and went about their merry way. Technology has improved since then, but the underlying principles have not evolved very much. We see something we like, discover it belongs to somebody else, and blow shit up until they give it to us. Or until there's nothing left—whichever comes first. It's quite eloquent in its simplicity.

With the ever-present threat of warfare looming overhead, one would think everyone would be holed up in bomb shelters all day. Yet day after day, humans go about their lives as if the world weren't likely to end tomorrow. Some would call this admirable; others would call it idiocy. Both would be right.

Our bombs are smarter than the average high school student. At least they can find Kuwait.

—ALAN WHITNEY BROWN, AMERICAN WRITER AND COMEDIAN

The archetypal fantasy-sports player feels that winning at fantasy says something about them.

—DON LEVY, AUSTRALIAN ARTIST AND FILM-MAKER

Oh, that. I just do that for the extra money, and to satisfy my male need to kill and win.

—CHARLIE SHEEN

Man has always assumed that he was more intelligent than dolphins because he had achieved so much ... the wheel, New York, wars, and so on ... while all the dolphins had ever done was muck about in the water having a good time. But conversely, the dolphins had always believed that they were far more intelligent than man ... for precisely the same reason.

—DOUGLAS ADAMS, BRITISH WRITER AND AUTHOR OF THE *HITCHHIKER'S GUIDE TO THE GALAXY* RADIO SERIES AND SUBSEQUENT NOVELS

If we don't succeed, we run the risk of failure.

—DAN QUAYLE

They misunderestimated me.

—GEORGE W. BUSH

To say that war is madness is like saying that sex is madness: true enough, from the standpoint of a stateless eunuch, but merely a provocative epigram for those who must make their arrangements in the world as given.

—JOHN UPDIKE,
AMERICAN NOVELIST

Some men are born mediocre, some men achieve mediocrity, and some men have mediocrity thrust upon them.

—JOSEPH HELLER, AMERICAN
NOVELIST, FROM *CATCH-22*

Never interrupt your enemy when he is making a mistake.

—NAPOLEON BONAPARTE

The whole art of war consists of guessing at what is on the other side of the hill.

—ARTHUR WELLESLEY, BRITISH
SOLDIER AND STATESMAN

Whether it's two kids fighting over a ball on the playground, or two adults fighting over decaying dinosaur remains, any dispute is ultimately a confrontation between people. And such confrontations are often more complicated than one party being right and the other being wrong. There are complicated emotional factors that come into play. One group may want to kill another, but what if that other group isn't ready to die just yet? This is why many people choose to discuss the limitations of human interaction rather than attempt to engage in them.

This is the devilish thing about foreign affairs: They are foreign and will not always conform to our whim.

—JAMES RESTON,
AMERICAN JOURNALIST

The problem with America today is that too many people know too much about not enough.

—MARGARET MEAD

The direct use of force is such a poor solution to any problem, it is generally employed only by small children and large nations.

—DAVID FRIEDMAN,
AMERICAN AUTHOR

Never underestimate the power of human stupidity.

—ROBERT A. HEINLEIN, AMERICAN SCIENCE FICTION AUTHOR

I would rather have an inferiority complex and be pleasantly surprised, than have a superiority complex and be rudely awakened.

—VANNA BONTA,
AMERICAN WRITER

Stupidity is a personal achievement which transcends national boundaries.

—ALBERT EINSTEIN

War is God's way of teaching Americans geography.

—AMBROSE BIERCE,
AMERICAN WRITER AND AUTHOR
OF THE DEVIL'S DICTIONARY

Men love war because it allows them to look serious. Because it is the one thing that stops women from laughing at them.

—JOHN FOWLES,
BRITISH NOVELIST

Don't hit at all if it is honorably possible to avoid hitting, but never hit soft.

—THEODORE ROOSEVELT

A prisoner of war is a man who tries to kill you and fails, and then asks you not to kill him.

—WINSTON CHURCHILL

While it is common to attack people on the other side of the planet, it is far more convenient to battle the pricks who live next door. First and foremost, they are infinitely closer. Second, they've probably been planning to do the same to you for years and it's best to beat them to the punch. While many cultures frown upon this practice, those are rarely the ones that last very long.

The supreme satisfaction is to be able to despise one's neighbor, and this fact goes far to account for religious intolerance. It is evidently consoling to reflect that the people next door are headed for hell.

—ALEISTER CROWLEY,
BRITISH THEOLOGIAN

A good neighbor is a fellow who smiles at you over the back fence, but doesn't climb over it.

—ARTHUR BAER,
AMERICAN JOURNALIST

It is easier to love human-ity as a whole than to love one's neighbor.

—ERIC HOFFER,
AMERICAN PHILOSOPHER

My neighbor asked if he could use my lawn mower, and I told him of course he could, so long as he didn't take it out of my garden.

—ERIC MORECAMBE,
BRITISH COMEDIAN

The Bible tells us to love our neighbors, and also to love our enemies; probably because they are generally the same people.

—G. K. Chesterton,
British writer

Every man is surrounded by a neighborhood of voluntary spies.

—Jane Austen

If you want to annoy your neighbors, tell the truth about them.

—Pietro Aretino,
Italian author

Good fences make good neighbors.

—Robert Frost

While some world leaders are strong, muscular individuals, the vast majority are old, decrepit bastards. This, coupled with the difficulty of conquering nations by oneself, makes amassing an army a necessity. As any warmonger can attest, having an army completely changes the game. Demands that once seemed crazy suddenly become reasonable. Countries that used to shun you now want to be best friends. If you've ever owned a gun, you sort of know the feeling. Just multiply it by 10 million.

Nothing so comforts the military mind as the maxim of a great but dead general.

—Barbara W. Tuchman,
World War I historian

Being in the army is like being in the Boy Scouts, except that the Boy Scouts have adult supervision.

—Farmer Fran,
The Waterboy

I don't know what effect these men will have upon the enemy, but, by God, they terrify me.

—Duke of Wellington

Without discipline the army would just be a bunch of guys wearing the same-color clothing.

—FRANK BURNS, *M*A*S*H*

After a hard day of basic training, you could eat a rattlesnake.

—ELVIS PRESLEY

If my soldiers were to begin to think, not one of them would remain in the army.

—FREDERICK II

An army of asses led by a lion is better than an army of lions led by an ass.

—GEORGE WASHINGTON

War is too serious a matter to entrust to military men.

—GEORGES CLEMENCEAU, FRENCH STATESMAN

Why can't they have gay people in the army? Personally, I think they are just afraid of a thousand guys with M16s going, "Who'd you call a faggot?"

—JON STEWART, AMERICAN POLITICAL SATIRIST

A soldier will fight long and hard for a bit of colored ribbon.

—NAPOLEON BONAPARTE

Considering all the unpleasant side effects of war—famine, disease, death, patriotism—it's surprising to learn there are those who can't get enough of it. Instead of going to war to live, some a**holes live to go to war. One could easily write them off as crazy, but upon further inspection their misguided obsession makes perfect sense. The vast majority of these warmongers never get within 1,000 miles of a real war. If they did, it's unlikely they'd survive long enough to change their minds.

To establish any mode to abolish war, however advantageous it might be to Nations, would be to take from such Government the most lucrative of its branches.

—THOMAS PAINE,
AMERICAN JOURNALIST AND
FOUNDING FATHER

The object of war is not to die for your country but to make the other bastard die for his.

—GEORGE S. PATTON

When I take action, I'm not going to fire a $2 million missile at a $10 empty tent and hit a camel in the butt. It's going to be decisive.

—GEORGE W. BUSH

My feelings—as usual—we will slaughter them all.

—MOHAMMED SAEED AL-SAHAF,
IRAQI DIPLOMAT AND
POLITICIAN

My fellow Americans, I am pleased to tell you I just signed legislation which outlaws Russia forever. The bombing will begin in five minutes.

—RONALD REAGAN,
WHILE PERFORMING A
MICROPHONE TEST

Once he has vanquished the final foe, the victorious general can finally claim his prize: a burning wasteland of famine and pestilence. It is at this point that he finally understands the true nature of war. It kind of sucks. And not in a "Damn, I spilled soup on my pants" sort of way. War sucks to such a magnitude that there is no word in any language capable of describing it, although that hasn't stopped a few scattered a**holes from trying.

Maybe this world is another planet's hell.

—ALDOUS HUXLEY,
BRITISH AUTHOR

You can no more win a war than you can win an earthquake.

—JEANNETTE RANKIN,
CONGRESSWOMAN

Fighting for peace is like screwing for virginity.

—GEORGE CARLIN,
AMERICAN COMEDIAN

Military intelligence is a contradiction in terms.

—Groucho Marx

Here's how bizarre the war is that we're in in Iraq, and we should have known this right from the get-go: When we first went into Iraq, Germany didn't want to go. Germany. The Michael Jordan of war took a pass.

—Jon Stewart,
American political satirist

It will be a great day when our schools have all the money they need, and our air force has to have a bake sale to buy a bomber.

—Robert Fulghum,
American author

War begins like a pretty girl with whom every man wants to flirt and ends like an ugly old woman whose visitors suffer and weep.

—Samuel HaNagid,
Spanish Talmudic scholar

After mucking about with the unpleasant practice of war for several millennia, a few forward-thinking individuals wondered what would happen if they refused to fight. While most were immediately killed, the trend started to gain traction and eventually humans stopped trying to beat each other senseless. Unfortunately they soon tired of peace and went back to hacking away at each other.

While the natural human state has always been one of constant warfare, small pockets of peace do pop up from time to time. It's just that nobody ever talks about it, for fear it will inspire everyone to start fighting again.

I believe in compulsory cannibalism. If people were forced to eat what they killed, there would be no more wars.

—Abbie Hoffman,
cofounder of the Youth
International Party

No country has suf-

fered so much from

the ruins of war

while being at peace

as the American.

—Edward Dahlberg,
American novelist

I come in peace. I didn't bring
artillery. But I'm pleading with
you, with tears in my eyes: If you
fuck with me, I'll kill you all.

—James Mattis,
United States Marine
Corps General

We must respect the other fellow's
religion, but only in the sense and
to the extent that we respect his
theory that his wife is beautiful
and his children smart.

—H. L. Mencken,
American journalist

Forgive your enemies, but never
forget their names.

—John F. Kennedy

Everyone's a pacifist between
wars. It's like being a vegetarian
between meals.

—Colman McCarthy,
American journalist
and lecturer

My hope is that gays will be running the world, because then there
would be no war. Just a greater
emphasis on military apparel.

—Roseanne Barr

THE QUOTABLE A**HOLE

CHAPTER 15

POLITICS

Wherever there exists a group of people coexisting peacefully, you can rest assured that things are one misstep away from going to complete and utter shit. There's no telling when it will happen, but eventually somebody will suggest that some rules to live by are a necessity. Then, of course, they need to think of penalties for people who ignore the rules. Inevitably a few people will decide the rules are stupid and offer to rewrite them. After some arguing over who should have the honor, two candidates will arise that our ill-fated citizens will get to vote on. Without even realizing it, our utopian society has invented politics—and their own undoing.

Regardless of the political system you live under, chances are you aren't too thrilled with the results. This is nothing to be alarmed about, as just about every human in history feels exactly the same way, and apart from the weather and sports, politics is the one thing a**holes like to talk about most.

I hate all bungling as I do sin, but particularly bungling in politics, which leads to the misery and ruin of many thousands and millions of people.

—JOHANN WOLFGANG VON
GOETHE, GERMAN WRITER

Crime does not pay . . . as well as politics.

—ALFRED E. NEUMAN,
MASCOT FOR *MAD MAGAZINE*

The ideal form of government is democracy tempered with assassination.

—VOLTAIRE,
FRENCH PHILOSOPHER

A public-opinion poll is no substitute for thought.

—WARREN BUFFETT,
AMERICAN BUSINESSMAN

I love to go to Washington—if only to be near my money.

—BOB HOPE

The only way I can lose this election is if I'm caught in bed with a dead girl or a live boy.

—EDWIN EDWARDS, FORMER
GOVERNOR OF LOUISIANA

Practical politics consists in ignoring facts.

—HENRY ADAMS, AMERICAN
JOURNALIST AND GRANDSON TO
JOHN QUINCY ADAMS

A sincere diplomat is like dry water or wooden iron.

—JOSEPH STALIN

Politics is the skilled use of blunt objects.

—LESTER BOWLES PEARSON,
CANADIAN HISTORIAN
AND POLITICIAN

In general, the art of government consists in taking as much money as possible from one party of the citizens to give to the other.

—VOLTAIRE,
FRENCH PHILOSOPHER

Humanity has invented a number of political systems over the years, and this alone foreshadows their inevitable shortcomings. If even one of them was any good, there wouldn't be a need for the others. But we have to work with what we've got, even if it isn't much.

While it's true your options for political activism are limited under certain forms of government, it's still important to get out there and pay lip service to the system. If nothing else, it will give you the right to bitch about it later when things don't turn out as well as you would have liked.

One of the penalties for refusing to participate in politics is that you end up being governed by your inferiors.

—PLATO

Strange women lying in ponds distributing swords is no basis for a system of government!

—DENNIS, *MONTY PYTHON AND THE HOLY GRAIL*

Democracy is being allowed to vote for the candidate you dislike least.

—ROBERT BYRNE,
AMERICAN PROFESSIONAL POOL
PLAYER AND AUTHOR

Communism is like prohibition: It's a good idea, but it won't work.

—WILL ROGERS,
AMERICAN COMEDIAN AND ACTOR

What is a committee? A group of the unwilling, picked from the unfit, to do the unnecessary.

—RICHARD HARKNESS,
AMERICAN JOURNALIST

Politics is perhaps the only profession for which no preparation is thought necessary.

—ROBERT LOUIS STEVENSON

Whether we and our politicians know it or not, Nature is party to all our deals and decisions, and she has more votes, a longer memory, and a sterner sense of justice than we do.

—WENDELL BERRY, AMERICAN WRITER

Instead of giving a politician the keys to the city, it might be better to change the locks.

—DOUG LARSON, AMERICAN COLUMNIST

The beautiful thing about democratic political systems is that they carry with them an inherent choice. Not the decision to vote for one dickhead over another, as this is merely an illusion anyway. The real choice is whether to convince yourself that your involvement matters, or to ignore anything and everything even remotely related to politics.

Regardless of your choice, the outcome is usually the same. Some a**hole who didn't deserve to be in power will wind up there. Everyone who voted for him will complain he's not keeping his promises, and everyone who didn't will say I told you so.

There is no act of treachery or meanness of which a political party is not capable; for in politics there is no honor.

—BENJAMIN DISRAELI, FORMER BRITISH PRIME MINISTER

Any party which takes credit for the rain must not be surprised if its opponents blame it for the drought.

—DWIGHT MORROW, UNITED STATES SENATOR

Reader, suppose you were an idiot; and suppose you were a member of Congress; but I repeat myself.

—MARK TWAIN

We'd all like to vote for the best man, but he's never a candidate.

—FRANK MCKINNEY "KIN" HUBBARD, AMERICAN CARTOONIST

If the gods had intended for people to vote, they would have given us candidates.

—HOWARD ZINN, AMERICAN HISTORIAN

A committee is a group of people who individually can do nothing but together can decide that nothing can be done.

—FRED ALLEN, AMERICAN COMEDIAN

The only means of strengthening one's intellect is to make up one's mind about nothing / to let the mind be a thoroughfare for all thoughts. Not a select party.

—JOHN KEATS

You can lead a man to Congress, but you can't make him think.

—MILTON BERLE, AMERICAN COMEDIAN AND ACTOR

To succeed inside a political party, one must cultivate an ability to sit still and remain polite while foolish people speak nonsense.

—MORTON BLACKWELL, REPUBLICAN ACTIVIST

Criticizing a politician for being corrupt is a lot like scolding your dog for shitting on the carpet. He knows you are mad about something, but your chances of getting him to understand what are slim. Despite the obvious futility, people continue to point fingers and hold protests in the hopes of altering the political landscape. While this might earn you a spot on the local evening news, shoving wads of cash in their pockets has proven much more effective. But if you don't have wads of cash available, bitching about them— while ultimately ineffective—can still be therapeutic.

The magician and the politician have much in common: They both have to draw our attention away from what they are really doing.

—BEN OKRI, NIGERIAN POET

You have all the characteristics of a popular politician: a horrible voice, bad breeding, and a vulgar manner.

—ARISTOPHANES

He knows nothing and thinks he knows everything. That points clearly to a political career.

—GEORGE BERNARD SHAW, IRISH PLAYWRIGHT AND AUTHOR

If there's anything a public servant hates to do, it's something for the public.

—FRANK MCKINNEY "KIN" HUBBARD, AMERICAN CARTOONIST

In Mexico, an air conditioner is called a "politician," because it makes a lot of noise but doesn't work very well.

—LEN DEIGHTON, BRITISH HISTORIAN

You want a friend in Washington? Get a dog.

—HARRY S. TRUMAN

When dealing with politicians, it is important to never mistake stupidity for conspiracy. While it's true some politicians do line their pants pockets with ill-gotten money, a large percentage of them lack the intelligence necessary to put on pants in the first place. So before you start railing against the corrupt suits in Washington, perhaps it would be wise to save your breath. Or at the very least put it in terms your congressman can understand. Preferably using stick figures and bright colors.

He never chooses an opinion; he just wears whatever happens to be in style.

—LEO TOLSTOY

Politics is just show business for ugly people.

—Jay Leno

Some fellows get credit for being conservative when they are only stupid.

—Frank McKinney "Kin" Hubbard, American cartoonist

Politicians are the same all over. They promise to build bridges even when there are no rivers.

—Nikita Khrushchev, former First Secretary of the Communist Party of the Soviet Union and successor to Joseph Stalin

You get fifteen Democrats in a room, and you get twenty opinions.

—Patrick Leahy, Vermont senator

Frankly, I'm suspicious of anyone who has a strong opinion on a complicated issue.

—Scott Adams, American cartoonist and creater of the *Dilbert* comics

Politicians are like diapers. They both need changing regularly and for the same reason.

—Unknown

Brains, you know, are suspect in the Republican Party.

—Walter Lippmann, American writer and political commentator

The reason there are two senators for each state is so that one can be the designated driver.

—Jay Leno

There ought to be one day—just one—when there is open season on senators.

—Will Rogers, American comedian and actor

At the end of the day, politics is supposed to be a serious business. The people we elect to office can literally destroy the world—or save it—depending on the decisions they make. So why do their antics continuously play out like characters on a daytime soap opera? From torrid love affairs in bathroom stalls to secret wiretaps and money laundering, politicians don't inspire much in the way of confidence. If they spent half as much time running the country as they do covering up their indiscretions, we might actually make some progress.

The Supreme Court has ruled that they cannot have a nativity scene in Washington, D.C. This wasn't for any religious reasons. They couldn't find three wise men and a virgin.

—JAY LENO

Oh, I don't blame Congress. If I had $600 billion at my disposal, I'd be irresponsible, too.

—GEORGE LICHTY,
AMERICAN CARTOONIST

Any political party that includes the word *democratic* in its name, isn't.

—PATRICK MURRAY,
AMERICAN POLITICIAN

If Thomas Jefferson thought taxation without representation was bad, he should see how it is with representation.

—RUSH LIMBAUGH,
AMERICAN CONSERVATIVE
RADIO PERSONALITY

There's no trick to being a humorist when you have the whole government working for you.

—WILL ROGERS, AMERICAN
COMEDIAN AND ACTOR

The problem with political jokes is that they get elected.

—GEORGE BERNARD SHAW,
IRISH PLAYWRIGHT AND AUTHOR

In America, anybody can be president. That's one of the risks you take.

—ADLAI STEVENSON, FORMER
GOVERNOR OF ILLINOIS

Of all the political positions available, none is so coveted as president of the United States. It's the most powerful position in the free world, so it's no surprise that it attracts some of the biggest a**holes, douche bags, and dickheads America has to offer.

Every four years we are presented with a cornucopia of candidates, which then gets widdled down to two—than one—viable a**holes. It's an elegant system, that inevitably results in 51 percent of the country getting what it wanted and 49 percent bitching about it for another four years. It may not be perfect, but for now it's all we've got.

Americans have different ways of saying things. They say elevator, we say lift . . . they say president, we say stupid psychopathic git.

—ALEXAI SAYLE,
BRITISH COMEDIAN

When I was a boy, I was told that anybody could become president; I'm beginning to believe it.

—CLARENCE SEWARD DARROW,
AMERICAN LAWYER FAMOUS FOR
HIS DEFENSE OF JOHN T. SCOPES
IN THE "SCOPES MONKEY TRIAL"

When the president does it, that means it's not illegal.

—RICHARD NIXON

The man with the best job in the country is the vice president. All he has to do is get up every morning and say, "How is the president?"

—WILL ROGERS, AMERICAN
COMEDIAN AND ACTOR

Folks, the president needs a break. He's like a Black & Decker cordless Dirt Devil vacuum. If you don't recharge his batteries, he can't suck.

—STEPHEN COLBERT,
AMERICAN POLITICAL SATIRIST

Because American kids are told from an early age that the United States is the greatest nation on earth, many are shocked to discover this might not be the case. In fact, there are 195 other entities that might beg to differ.

In general, Americans don't do so well in the rest of the world. The countries we aren't actively at war with tend to regard us as an insecure playground bully hell-bent on stealing everyone's toys. While it may be tempting to write them off, the wiser course of action might be to try listening to what they have to say. That way, it will be even more devastating when we inevitably invade.

I am not fond of speaking about politics because I don't have in my possession an army of 200,000 soldiers.

—FRANZ LISZT,
HUNGARIAN COMPOSER

Freedom is just chaos, with better lighting.

—ALAN DEAN FOSTER,
AMERICAN SCIENCE-FICTION
WRITER AND AUTHOR OF THE
ORIGINAL STAR WARS NOVEL

I have discovered the art of deceiving diplomats. I tell them the truth and they never believe me.

—CAMILLO DI CAVOUR,
ITALIAN PRIME MINISTER

A government that robs Peter to pay Paul can always depend on the support of Paul.

—GEORGE BERNARD SHAW,
IRISH PLAYWRIGHT AND AUTHOR

Under democracy one party always devotes its chief energies to trying to prove that the other party is unfit to rule—and both commonly succeed, and are right.

—H. L. MENCKEN,
AMERICAN JOURNALIST

Socialism never took root in America because the poor see themselves not as an exploited proletariat but as temporarily embarrassed millionaires.

—JOHN STEINBECK

Every marriage of an intellectual with the Communist Party ends in adultery.

—NICOLÁS GÓMEZ DÁVILA,
COLOMBIAN WRITER

A diplomat is a man who always remembers a woman's birthday but never remembers her age.

—ROBERT FROST

I think it would be a good idea.

—MAHATMA GANDHI, WHEN
ASKED WHAT HE THOUGHT OF
WESTERN CIVILIZATION

PART 5

THE OPPOSITE
SEX

Sometimes I wonder if men and women really suit each other. Perhaps they should live next door and just visit now and then.

—Katharine Hepburn

CHAPTER 16

DATING

No one ever said that dating was easy. In fact, it can be freaking scary out there. Every time you step out of your door looking for true love, you face embarrassment, stupidity, and humanity's biggest fear: rejection.

But even if the object of your affection agrees to go out with you, you're still not in the clear. Even successful courtships bring with them a host of uncomfortable situations full of awkward silences and uncontrollable back sweat. But regardless of how absurd or complex the situation, you'll feel better when you realize that others have been there before you and have handled dating with ineptitude, disgrace, and a fair amount of biting sarcasm that only history's greatest a**holes can provide.

What do these dicks have to say about dating? You'll find a whole conversation in this chapter, but let's start here.

How many of you have ever started dating because you were too lazy to commit suicide?

—JUDY TENUTA,
AMERICAN COMEDIAN

I love you like a fat kid loves cake.

—50 CENT,
AMERICAN RAP ARTIST

To be trusted is a greater compliment than being loved.

—GEORGE MACDONALD,
SCOTTISH FANTASY AUTHOR

Basically we are descended from a long line of successful flirts and it is hard-wired into our brains. If we didn't initiate contact with the opposite sex, then we wouldn't reproduce, and the species would die out.

—KATE FOX, BRITISH
SOCIAL ANTHROPOLOGIST

There is always some madness in love. But there is also always some reason in madness.

—FRIEDRICH NIETZSCHE

Watching your daughter being collected by her date feels like handing over a $1 million Stradivarius to a gorilla.

—JIM BISHOP,
AMERICAN JOURNALIST

You have to walk carefully in the beginning of love; the running across fields into your lover's arms can only come later when you're sure they won't laugh if you trip.

—JONATHAN CARROLL,
AMERICAN AUTHOR

I'm selfish, impatient, and a little insecure. I make mistakes, I am out of control and at times hard to handle. But if you can't handle me at my worst, then you sure as hell don't deserve me at my best.

—MARILYN MONROE

Kissing is a means of getting two people so close together that they can't see anything wrong with each other.

—RENE YASENEK

I married the first man I ever kissed. When I tell this to my children, they just about throw up.

—BARBARA BUSH

No one will win the battle of the sexes; there is too much flirting with the enemy.

—HENRY KISSINGER,
AMERICAN DIPLOMAT

If you use television and movies as your guide, dating seems pretty easy. All you have to do is meet a socially awkward person, master some obscure hobby he or she finds attractive, and live happily ever after. This is, of course, nothing at all what dating's really like. If they made an honest movie about dating, it would be ten minutes long. The couple meets, then cut to them watching TV on separate couches. One of them farts and the other laughs and says, "This isn't working." Roll credits. So perhaps you should save yourself the trouble of getting romantically involved and read about it instead.

Every relationship is fundamentally a power struggle, and the individual in power is whoever likes the other person less.

—CHUCK KLOSTERMAN,
AMERICAN WRITER

Do not let a flattering woman coax and wheedle you and deceive you; she is after your barn.

—HESIOD, GREEK POET

Love is hiding who you really are at all times. Even when you're sleeping. Love is wearing makeup to bed, and going downstairs to the Burger King to poop. And hiding alcohol in perfume bottles. That's love.

—JENNA MARONEY, *30 ROCK*

Every man's dream is to be able to sink into the arms of a woman without also falling into her hands.

—JERRY LEWIS

Love is all fun and games until someone loses an eye or gets pregnant.

—JIM COLE, AMERICAN
COLLEGE FOOTBALL COACH

Love is like racing across the frozen tundra on a snowmobile which flips over, trapping you underneath. At night, the ice weasels come.

—MATT GROENING,
AMERICAN CARTOONIST AND
CREATOR OF *THE SIMPSONS*

Love is a serious mental disease.

—PLATO

While it can be difficult to describe the process of falling in love, it might be helpful to think of it like this: Imagine staring into a concrete pool where the water has been replaced with live wolverines and all the lifeguards look like those kids from *Children of the Corn*. Yet despite the inherent risk, you dive in anyway.

There is not a single person on earth who would ever advise another to fall in love. In fact, quite the opposite is true. Yet somehow it keeps happening. Before you go running off into the sunset in search of affection, you might want to listen to those who failed before you.

Love is two minds

without a single

thought.

—PHILIP BARRY,
AMERICAN PLAYWRIGHT

The difference between friend-ship and love is how much you can hurt each other.

—Ashleigh Brilliant,
American cartoonist

Never go to bed mad—stay up and fight.

—Phyllis Diller, American
comedian and actress

Love is like an hourglass, with the heart filling up as the brain empties.

—Jules Renard,
French author

Love is like wine: To sip is fine, but to empty the bottle is a headache.

—Julio Iglesias,
Spanish singer

When you fish for love, bait with your heart, not your brain.

—Mark Twain

Despite what some people would have you believe, men are still a necessary variable when seeking to propagate the human race. And we should be thankful for that fact, because otherwise it's unlikely women would keep us around for very long.

Men are good at many things, but being thoughtful, attentive mates is not one of them. And barring competition from a third-party candidate, it's unlikely we are going to change anytime soon. While most women simply roll their eyes and soldier on, there are some willing to put us in our place.

Mr. Right is coming. But he's in Africa and he's walking.

—Oprah Winfrey

The male is a domestic animal which, if treated with firmness and kindness, can be trained to do most things.

—JILLY COOPER,
BRITISH AUTHOR

Being a woman is a terribly difficult task since it consists principally in dealing with men.

—JOSEPH CONRAD

Women want mediocre men. And men are working hard to become as mediocre as possible.

—MARGARET MEAD

Can you imagine a world without men? No crime and lots of happy, fat women.

—MARION SMITH,
AMERICAN AUTHOR

Male menopause is a lot more fun than female menopause. With female menopause you gain weight and get hot flashes. Male menopause—you get to date young girls and drive motorcycles.

—RITA RUDNER, AMERICAN
ACTRESS AND COMEDIAN

Though we adore men individually, we agree that as a group they're rather stupid.

—MRS. BANKS, MARY POPPINS

For as awful as men are at interspecies interactions, women are not without faults of their own. When they aren't busy grinding men's hearts into a bloody pulp, they can be moody, indecisive, needy, shallow, and controlling— and those are their good qualities.

Yet time and time again, men jump from one woman to another, convinced that the next one will be different. That we will finally find a girl who can overlook our meager bank account and expanding waistline and love us for who we are. Sadly, nine times out of ten, this fruitless search ends in frustrated name-calling, as evidenced by the following a**holes.

The problem with most men is they're a**holes. The problem with most women is they put up with those a**holes.

—CHER

When a young man complains that a young lady has no heart, it's pretty certain that she has his.

—GEORGE DENNISON PRENTICE, AMERICAN JOURNALIST

She was the kind of girl who'd eat all your cashews and leave you with nothing but peanuts and filberts.

—RAYMOND CHANDLER, AMERICAN NOVELIST

Girls are like slugs. They serve some purpose, but it's hard to imagine what.

—CALVIN, *CALVIN AND HOBBES*

There are only three things women need in life: food, water, and compliments.

—CHRIS ROCK, AMERICAN COMEDIAN

Any girl can be glamorous. All you have to do is stand still and look stupid.

—HEDY LAMARR, AUSTRIAN ACTRESS

Biologically speaking, if something bites you, it is more likely to be female.

—DESMOND MORRIS, BRITISH ZOOLOGIST

To be happy with a man, you must understand him a lot and love him a little. To be happy with a woman, you must love her a lot and not try to understand her at all.

—HELEN ROWLAND, AMERICAN JOURNALIST

A woman's mind is cleaner than a man's. She changes it more often.

—OLIVER HERFORD, AMERICAN WRITER AND ILLUSTRATOR

A woman will lie about anything, just to stay in practice.

—PHILIP MARLOWE,
THE LONG GOODBYE

Women and cats will do as they please, and men and dogs should relax and get used to the idea.

—ROBERT A. HEINLEIN, AMERI-
CAN SCIENCE FICTION AUTHOR

Women's intuition is the result of millions of years of not thinking.

—RUPERT HUGHES,
AMERICAN HISTORIAN

When you've exhausted the traditional dating channels of casual bar encounters and awkward exchanges at the grocery store, the option of online dating is a ray of hope in an otherwise desolate field of desperation and loneliness. But as you sift through a sea of potential mates, keep in mind that what you see is not necessarily what you get. The camera may add 10 pounds, but it can also take away 200 with the proper use of angles and dim lighting. So before you enter into the world of online dating, be prepared with what to say in case your date looks less like the pictures you saw online and more like a sunburned walrus.

You're looking exceptionally ugly tonight, Madam; is it because we have company?

—ALFRED JARRY,
FRENCH WRITER

To lengthen thy life, lessen thy meals.

—BENJAMIN FRANKLIN

I do not know if she was virtuous, but she was ugly, and with a woman that is half the battle.

—HEINRICH HEINE,
GERMAN POET

Some cause happiness wherever they go; others whenever they go.

—OSCAR WILDE

I found there was only one way to look thin: Hang out with fat people.

—Rodney Dangerfield,
American comedian

A fat stomach never breeds fine thoughts.

—Saint Jerome

I've been on so many blind dates, I should get a free dog.

—Wendy Liebman,
American comedian

O, she is the antidote to desire.

—William Congreve,
English playwright and poet

Beauty is only skin-deep, but ugly goes clean to the bone.

—Dorothy Parker,
American poet

Since we were kids, we were spoon-fed the notion that there is someone out there for everyone. No matter how ugly and deformed you happen to be, if you are beautiful on the inside, you will find true love . . .

Kids are so gullible.

The truth is that there are plenty of people out there who are completely undatable. On the outskirts of society lives a subsect of forever-alone mouth-breathers. Since they have no one to date, they busy themselves playing World of Warcraft and knitting miniature cat sweaters in complete and utter solitude. But before you take pity on them, think about all the heartache they will never experience and all the extra money sitting in their bank account, and ask yourself, "Who is the sucker now?"

All alone! Whether you like it or not, alone is something you'll be quite a lot.

—Dr. Seuss

Don't knock masturbation. It's sex with someone I love.

—WOODY ALLEN

An intellectual is someone who has found something more interesting than sex.

—EDGAR WALLACE,
BRITISH NOVELIST

It is easy for me to love myself, but for ladies to do it is another question altogether.

—JOHNNY VEGAS,
BRITISH COMEDIAN

We have reason to believe that man first walked upright to free his hands for masturbation.

—LILY TOMLIN

For birth control, I rely on my personality.

—MILT ABEL,
AMERICAN COMEDIAN

If you are not too long, I will wait here for you all my life.

—OSCAR WILDE

The love that lasts the longest is the love that is never returned.

—W. SOMERSET MAUGHAM,
BRITISH PLAYWRIGHT

CHAPTER 17

GETTING LAID

While long walks on the beach and romantic evenings reciting poetry can be nice, for most a**holes they are merely a means to an end. If they had it their way, most dates would skip straight from the introduction to the bedroom. It's not that a**holes don't want to get to know you first; it's just that doing so is not really going to affect their desired outcome. And while most a**holes keep their true intentions a carefully guarded secret, some have been kind enough to reveal their real feelings about their sexual misadventures.

The only reason to wait a month for sex is if she's seventeen years, eleven months old.

—BARNEY STINSON,
HOW I MET YOUR MOTHER

Son, a woman is like a beer. They smell good, they look good, you'd step over your own mother just to get one! But you can't stop at one. You wanna drink another woman!

—HOMER J. SIMPSON,
THE SIMPSONS

Sex education may be a good idea in the schools, but I don't believe the kids should be given homework.

—BILL COSBY

I blame my mother for my poor sex life. All she told me was "The man goes on top and the woman underneath." For three years my husband and I slept in bunk beds.

—JOAN RIVERS

Girls are much more psychic than guys. They're the first to know if you're going to get laid.

—PAUL RODRIGUEZ,
MEXICAN COMEDIAN AND ACTOR

Men reach their sexual peak at eighteen. Women reach theirs at thirty-five. Do you get the feeling that God is playing a practical joke?

—RITA RUDNER, AMERICAN
ACTRESS AND COMEDIAN

The big difference between sex for money and sex for free is that sex for money usually costs a lot less.

—BRENDAN BEHAN,
IRISH AUTHOR

Give me chastity and continence, but not yet!

—SAINT AUGUSTINE

There is a time and a place for expressing your feelings. Like when your dog dies or somebody cuts you off in traffic. But the last place you should ever get emotional is in the bedroom. Because nothing can kill the mood faster than uncontrollable sobbing— even if the tears are tears of happiness.

Sometimes sex is just sex. Two people (or sometimes more) were horny at the same time and decided to do something about it. And God bless the brave individuals willing to admit it.

An orgasm a day keeps the doctor away.

—MAE WEST

This is an occasion for genuinely tiny knickers.

—BRIDGET JONES,
BRIDGET JONES'S DIARY

I don't pay them for sex. I pay them to leave.

—CHARLIE SHEEN

You know when you hear girls say, "Ah man, I was so shitfaced last night; I shouldn't have fucked that guy"? We could be that mistake!

—SETH, SUPERBAD

A man can be happy with any woman as long as he does not love her.

—OSCAR WILDE

I believe that sex is one of the most beautiful, natural, wholesome things that money can buy.

—STEVE MARTIN

A hard man is good to find.

—MAE WEST

The sex life of the average human is a lot like a baseball game: lots of sitting around waiting for something to happen punctuated by brief moments of excitement. And when it's all over, you wish you'd just stayed at home and watched the game on TV. But then there are the select few whose sex lives are more like the Cirque du Soleil. Even weeks after going to the show, you're still not 100 percent sure exactly what you saw.

There's a reason it's called "girls gone wild" and not "women gone wild." When girls go wild, they show their tits. When women go wild, they kill men and drown their kids in a tub.

—LOUIS C. K.,
AMERICAN COMEDIAN

If I really got my ribs removed, I would have been busy sucking my own dick on *The Wonder Years* instead of chasing Winnie Cooper. Besides, I wouldn't have sucked other people's dicks on stage, either. I would have been sucking my own. Plus, who really has time to be killing puppies when you can be sucking your own dick? I think I'm gonna call the surgeon in the morning.

—MARILYN MANSON,
AMERICAN ROCK MUSICIAN

When the authorities warn you of the dangers of having sex, there is an important lesson to be learned. Do not have sex with the authorities.

—MATT GROENING,
AMERICAN CARTOONIST AND
CREATOR OF *THE SIMPSONS*

A lot of my peer group think I'm an eccentric bisexual, like I may even have an ammonia-filled tentacle somewhere on my body. That's okay.

—ROBERT DOWNEY JR.,
AMERICAN ACTOR

My own belief is that there is hardly anyone whose sexual life, if it were broadcast, would not fill the world at large with surprise and horror.

—W. SOMERSET MAUGHAM,
BRITISH PLAYWRIGHT

Remember, if you smoke after sex, you're doing it too fast.

—WOODY ALLEN

You know that when I hate you, it is because I love you to a point of passion that unhinges my soul.

—JULIE DE LESPINASSE,
EIGHTEENTH-CENTURY
FRENCH SOCIALITE

There is a secret about attracting potential partners that few people are privy to. You can be the baldest, fattest, ugliest beast on the planet, but if you act like you are God's gift to humanity, you will still get laid. Because as much as people are turned off by your unsightly acne scars and the malformed hump on your left shoulder, nothing turns people on more than confidence.

Anyone can be confident with a full head of hair. But a confident bald man—there's your diamond in the rough.

—LARRY DAVID,
AMERICAN COMEDIAN

A man can be short and dumpy and getting bald, but if he has fire, women will like him.

—MAE WEST

Dancing: the vertical expression of a horizontal desire.

—GEORGE BERNARD SHAW,
IRISH PLAYWRIGHT AND AUTHOR

A man's only as old as the woman he feels.

—GROUCHO MARX

Other people's opinion of you does not have to become your reality.

—LES BROWN, AMERICAN
MOTIVATIONAL SPEAKER

There are few things better than waking up after a night on the town to discover a half-naked stranger sharing your bed. Even if you can't remember what happened, it stands to reason things went well. But this feeling of elation can come to a screeching halt when he or she rolls over to reveal a being which may or may not actually be human. Although it's true you could have done better, it's important to remember that you are no prize yourself. At the end of the day, sex is sex—even if it might be considered bestiality in some states.

What are you gonna do for a face when the baboon wants his ass back?

—UNKNOWN

He had a big head and a face so ugly it became almost fascinating.

—AYN RAND, RUSSIAN NOVELIST

Beauty may be skin deep, but ugly goes clear to the bone.

—REDD FOXX,
AMERICAN COMEDIAN

At first I thought he was walking a dog. Then I realized it was his date.

—CUDDLES KOVINSKY,
POLYESTER

He had a winning smile, but everything else was a loser.

—GEORGE C. SCOTT,
AMERICAN ACTOR

I never forget a face, but in your case I'll make an exception.

—GROUCHO MARX

I could dance with you until the cows come home ... on second thoughts, I'll dance with the cows and you go home.

—GROUCHO MARX

She resembles the Venus de Milo: she is very old, has no teeth, and has white spots on her yellow skin.

—HEINRICH HEINE,
GERMAN POET

Last week I stated this woman was the ugliest woman I had ever seen. I have since been visited by her sister ... and now wish to withdraw that statement.

—MARK TWAIN

While some lucky individuals need merely bat their eyelashes or tousle their hair to attract potential suitors, most of us must engage in the ill-fated misadventure known as casual conversation. While you may experience limited success as long as you can form a complete sentence and avoid hyperventilating, inevitably your charm and wit will fall on deaf ears. Luckily, even if he or she is just not that into you, there are a plethora of retorts for when you strike out.

You are beautiful, but you are empty.

—ANTOINE DE SAINT-EXUPÉRY,
FRENCH WRITER

No one is more insufferable than he who lacks basic courtesy.

—BRYANT H. MCGILL,
AMERICAN AUTHOR

You're in pretty good shape for the shape you are in.

—DR. SEUSS

A whole page of learned polysyllables may not convey as much as the statement that a certain woman is a bitch, or that a certain man is a jerk.

—ERIC BERNE,
CANADIAN PSYCHIATRIST

She's so pure; Moses couldn't even part her knees.

—JOAN RIVERS

If you act like an a**hole one night, (you) might not remember it. But we will.

—ROB LORENC,
PROFESSIONAL BARTENDER

I know very little about acting. I'm just an incredibly gifted faker.

—ROBERT DOWNEY JR.,
AMERICAN ACTOR

A fast word about oral contraception. I asked a girl to go to bed with me and she said no.

—WOODY ALLEN

You're like a giant cock-blocking robot made by the government.

—COLUMBUS, ZOMBIELAND

You know that look women get when they want sex? Me neither.

—DREW CAREY,
AMERICAN COMEDIAN, ACTOR,
AND GAME SHOW HOST

It's no secret that men will sleep with anything that moves, but what most women don't realize is that men's standards are actually much lower than that. Movement is nice, but it is no way a prerequisite. In fact, there is almost no limit to how low men will lower their standards in the pursuit of sex. Especially if it's been a while. While it's easy to label men as pigs, this really isn't fair to such a noble animal. Calling men men is insult enough.

I wasn't kissing her. I was whispering in her mouth.

—CHICO MARX,
AMERICAN ACTOR AND BROTHER
OF GROUCHO MARX

The first thing men notice about a woman is her eyes. Then, when her eyes aren't looking, they notice her breasts.

—CONAN O'BRIEN,
AMERICAN COMEDIAN AND
LATE-NIGHT TELEVISION HOST

When I go to a bar, I don't go looking for a girl who knows the capital of Maine.

—DAVID BRENNER,
AMERICAN COMEDIAN

Only one man in a thousand is a leader of men, the other 999 follow women.

—GROUCHO MARX

No man has ever put his hand up a girl's dress looking for a library card.

—JOAN RIVERS

See, the problem is that God gives men a brain and a penis, and only enough blood to run one at a time.

—ROBIN WILLIAMS

I have an intense desire to return to the womb. Anybody's.

—WOODY ALLEN

When young women are growing up, their mother usually warns them that men are only interested in one thing. They aren't told exactly what that one thing is, just that they shouldn't give it to them. Fast-forward a few years and women finally figure out what that thing is. While some dutifully heed their mother's advice, a few give in to temptation to see what all the fuss is about. While they were right that men were only interested in sex, their mothers neglected to mention one important thing: Women have just as much right to be interested in only one thing as well.

Jesus said, "Love one another." He didn't say love the whole world.

—Mother Teresa

In order to avoid being called a flirt, she always yielded easily.

—Charles, Count Talleyrand, French diplomat

She wore too much rouge last night and not quite enough clothes. That is always a sign of despair in a woman.

—Oscar Wilde

If all the girls who attended the Harvard-Yale game were laid end to end, I wouldn't be surprised.

—Dorothy Parker, American poet

You were born with your legs apart. They'll send you to the grave in a Y-shaped coffin.

—Frederic Raphael, American writer

Desperate is not a sexual preference.

—RANDY K. MILHOLLAND,
AMERICAN CARTOONIST MOST
FAMOUS FOR THE WEBCOMIC,
SOMETHING POSITIVE

She has been kissed as often as a police-court Bible, and by much the same class of people.

—ROBERTSON DAVIES,
CANADIAN AUTHOR

That woman speaks eight languages and can't say no in any of them.

—DOROTHY PARKER,
AMERICAN POET

She's been on more laps than a napkin.

—WALTER WINCHELL,
AMERICAN COLUMNIST

I never expected to see the day when girls would get sunburned in the places they now do.

—WILL ROGERS, AMERICAN
COMEDIAN AND ACTOR

Until recently, men and women could engage in raucous unprotected sex with as many willing partners as they could find. Of course, this was back when the worst that could happen is it burned for a few weeks when you peed. Nowadays, having sex is riskier than smearing your naughty bits with honey and running naked through bear country. At least there's a chance you can outrun the bear.

With that in mind, perhaps it might be wise to plug in the old Xbox this weekend and spend some quality time alone. Your reproductive organs will thank you.

I have a love interest in every one of my films: a gun.

—ARNOLD SCHWARZENEGGER

He who loves fifty people has fifty woes; he who loves no one has no woes.

—BUDDHA

Why get married and make one man miserable when I can stay single and make thousands miserable?

—CARRIE SNOW,
AMERICAN COMEDIAN

Language . . . has created the word "loneliness" to express the pain of being alone. And it has created the word "solitude" to express the glory of being alone.

—PAUL TILLICH,
GERMAN PHILOSOPHER

I love Mickey Mouse more than any woman I have ever known.

—WALT DISNEY

If you love something, set it free. Just don't be surprised if it comes back with herpes.

—CHUCK PALAHNIUK,
AMERICAN NOVELIST

A woman is just a woman, but a good cigar is a smoke.

—RUDYARD KIPLING

CHAPTER 18

DUMPING

Until fairly recently, men and women had very few options when things turned sour. Women had no choice but to wait it out and hope they outlived their partner. Men had little choice but to expedite their mate's mortality themselves. Both sexes had the most popular option: to suck it up and pretend everything was fine. None of these are very good options when you'd rather chew your own hand off than spend another second with this person.

It wasn't until the concepts of dumping and divorce gained widespread approval that we were finally free to move around to our hearts' content. While nobody really enjoys getting dumped, it sure beats being smothered by a pillow.

Now getting kicked to the curb is a right of passage for every young man and women. It builds character and prepares you for the host of inevitable disappointments you are sure to face in the future. And if you are lucky, you may even have the privilege to do it yourself one day.

While it's true that one should never take pleasure inflicting emotional pain on others, that doesn't really apply if they deserve it. And even if they didn't do anything wrong, chances are, they would have eventually.

So no matter which end of the equation you fall on, dumpee or dumper, take comfort in the unkind words of these bitter, lovelorn a**holes.

I'm always fascinated by the way memory diffuses fact.

—DIANE SAWYER,
AMERICAN NEWS ANCHOR

I've never been married, but I tell people I'm divorced so they won't think something is wrong with me.

—ELAYNE BOOSLER, AMERICAN
ACTRESS AND COMEDIAN

Show me a woman who doesn't feel guilty and I'll show you a man.

—ERICA JONG,
AMERICAN AUTHOR

Why do you have to break up with her? Be a man. Just stop calling.

—JOEY, *FRIENDS*

Hatred is blind, as well as love.

—OSCAR WILDE

There is a good way to break up with someone and it doesn't include a Post-it.

—CARRIE, *SEX AND THE CITY*

It's relaxing to go out with my ex-wife because she already knows I'm an idiot.

—WARREN THOMAS,
AMERICAN COMEDIAN

Considering how awful the courtship process can be, it's understandable why most people would rather stay in a failing relationship than risk getting dumped. Sure, you don't love each other anymore and haven't slept together in months, but you'll be damned if you are going to start dating again.

But regardless of your efforts to maintain the status quo, at some point you will experience the cold, uncaring backhand of a breakup. I could tell you that it's not as bad as it sounds, but the following a**holes would disagree.

Goodbye. I am leaving because I am bored.

—GEORGE SANDERS,
RUSSIAN ACTOR

A guy can just as easily dump you if you fuck him on the first date as he can if you wait until the tenth.

—SAMANTHA, *SEX AND THE CITY*

You know what is the worst thing about being rejected? The lack of control. If I could only control the where and how of being dumped, it wouldn't seem as bad.

—ROB FLEMING, *HIGH FIDELITY*

Your heart is my piñata.

—CHUCK PALAHNIUK,
AMERICAN NOVELIST

Women might be able to fake orgasms, but men can fake whole relationships.

—SHARON STONE,
AMERICAN ACTRESS

There's a common misconception that it's possible for the person initiating the breakup to be the one with a problem. This is unequivocally false. The "It's me, not you" line is almost as absurd as the "Size doesn't matter" fallacy perpetuated by the society of men with small wangs. If you are being dumped, rest assured the other person thinks you either did something wrong or failed to do something right.

I will always love the false image I had of you.

—ASHLEIGH BRILLIANT,
AMERICAN CARTOONIST

Relationships are hard. It's like a full-time job, and we should treat it like one. If your boyfriend or girlfriend wants to leave you, they should give you two weeks' notice. There should be severance pay, and before they leave you, they should have to find you a temp.

—BOB ETTINGER,
AMERICAN COLUMNIST

A lot of beautiful people are stupid. There are a tremendous number of idiots who look so good. It's frightening.

—DEAN CAIN, AMERICAN ACTOR

Love is a state in which a man sees things most decidedly as they are not.

—FRIEDRICH NIETZSCHE

Once a woman has given you her heart, you can never get rid of the rest of her body.

—SIR JOHN VANBRUGH,
BRITISH ARCHITECT

How could I be sleeping with this peculiar man. . . . Surely only true love could justify my lack of taste.

—MARGARET ATWOOD,
CANADIAN AUTHOR

It's no good pretending that any relationship has a future if your record collections disagree violently or if your favorite films wouldn't even speak to each other if they met at a party.

—ROB FLEMING, *HIGH FIDELITY*

Every time I look at you, I get a fierce desire to be lonesome.

—OSCAR LEVANT, AMERICAN
MUSICIAN AND ACTOR

After a particularly devastating breakup, it is only natural to reflect on the relationship to try and pinpoint where things went south. If you can't recall any instances of infidelity or other glaring mistakes, perhaps the fact that you spent every Friday playing Scrabble and watching reruns of *CSI* didn't help.

Like all things, relationships get boring if you don't make an effort to keep things interesting. Whether it's dressing up to go out dancing or making out in the back of a movie theater, variety is the spice of life. Otherwise you'll wind up old and alone like these a**holes.

An affair now and then is good for a marriage. It adds spice, stops it from getting boring. . . . I ought to know.

—BETTE DAVIS

There's an innocence that has kind of gone away. Umm . . . the novelty factor hasn't been there for a while.

—CHARLIE SHEEN

My wife, Mary, and I have been married for forty-seven years and not once have we had an argument serious enough to consider divorce; murder, yes, but divorce, never.

—JACK BENNY,
AMERICAN COMEDIAN

I love to shop after a bad relationship. I don't know. I buy a new outfit and it makes me feel better. It just does. Sometimes if I see a really great outfit, I'll break up with someone on purpose.

—RITA RUDNER, AMERICAN
ACTRESS AND COMEDIAN

He was happily married—but his wife wasn't.

—VICTOR BORGE,
DANISH COMEDIAN

Men should be like Kleenex: soft, strong, and disposable.

—CHER

While nobody wants to believe their partner is capable of such treachery, the truth is a lot of people won't end an existing relationship until they have already secured plan B. And oddly enough, we're usually more interested in kicking plan B's teeth in than we are getting even with the a**hole who left us for it.

Unless you wrongly believed your partner was dead, there is absolutely no excuse for cheating. Unless, of course the person was really hot. Or you were really drunk. Or you were just kind of bored that night. On second thought, if the following a**holes are any indicator, cheating is perfectly acceptable.

Tell him I've been too fucking busy—or vice versa.

—DOROTHY PARKER,
AMERICAN POET

Your idea of fidelity is not having more than one man in bed at the same time.

—FREDERIC RAPHAEL,
AMERICAN WRITER

Why was I with her? She reminds me of you. In fact, she reminds me more of you than you do!

—GROUCHO MARX

An open marriage is nature's way of telling you that you need a divorce.

—ANN LANDERS

I've been in love with the same woman for forty-nine years. If my wife ever finds out, she'll kill me!

—HENNY YOUNGMAN,
BRITISH COMEDIAN

A man can sleep around no questions asked, but if a woman makes nineteen or twenty mistakes, she's a tramp.

—JOAN RIVERS

Don't keep a man guessing too long—he's sure to find the answer somewhere else.

—MAE WEST

Husbands are chiefly good lovers when they are betraying their wives.

—MARILYN MONROE

There were three of us in this marriage, so it was a bit crowded.

—PRINCESS DIANA

There is one thing I would break up over, and that is if she caught me with another woman. I won't stand for that.

—STEVE MARTIN

Eventually I became involved with somebody, and I was fired.

—TOMMY KIRK,
AMERICAN ACTOR

If you marry a man who cheats on his wife, you'll be married to a man who cheats on his wife.

—ANN LANDERS

While being dumped by a boyfriend or girlfriend may seem like the end of the world, at least you get to keep your house. If you made the monumental mistake of getting married first, you might not be so lucky.

Remember that box of stuff your significant other used to drop off as a consolation prize after a breakup? Well, a divorce is sort of like that, except you replace the box with an envelope and your stuff with a stack of papers detailing how much money you now owe the person who hates you most in the world.

The clearest explanation for the failure of any marriage is that the two people are incompatible; that is, one is male and the other female.

—ANNA QUINDLEN,
AMERICAN COLUMNIST

I never hated a man enough to give his diamonds back.

—ZSA ZSA GABOR

Alimony is like

buying oats for

a dead horse.

—ARTHUR BAER,
AMERICAN JOURNALIST

Alimony—the ransom that the happy pay to the devil.

—H. L. MENCKEN,
AMERICAN JOURNALIST

I don't think I'll get married again. I'll just find a woman I don't like and give her a house.

—LEWIS GRIZZARD,
AMERICAN COMEDIAN

Whenever I date a guy, I think, Is this the man I want my children to spend their weekends with?

—RITA RUDNER, AMERICAN ACTRESS AND COMEDIAN

Ah, yes, divorce . . . from the Latin word meaning to rip out a man's genitals through his wallet.

—ROBIN WILLIAMS

For a while we pondered whether to take a vacation or get a divorce. We decided that a trip to Bermuda is over in two weeks, but a divorce is something you always have.

—WOODY ALLEN

I am a marvelous housekeeper. Every time I leave a man I keep his house.

—ZSA ZSA GABOR

In Hollywood a marriage is a success if it outlasts milk.

—RITA RUDNER, AMERICAN ACTRESS AND COMEDIAN

You thought you had met the love of your life, but while you were busy naming your unborn children, she was busy thinking of ways to fake her own death to get out of it. But don't let it get you down. Things could always be worse. For one, she could have kept dating you.

By and large, getting dumped is the best thing that could possibly happen to somebody in a relationship. Just think of all the wonderful things you can start doing again. You can stay out late or drink beer in the shower. You can even leave the toilet seat up like nature intended! At the end of the day, you're always better off alone.

When a man steals your wife, there is no better revenge than to let him keep her.

—SACHA GUITRY, ACTOR AND DIRECTOR

A good relationship is like fire-works: loud, explosive, and liable to maim you if you hold on too long.

—JEPH JACQUES,
PRODUCER OF THE WEBCOMIC
QUESTIONABLE CONTENT

I broke up with someone, and she said, "You'll never find anyone like me again." And I'm thinking, "I hope not!" Does anybody end a bad relationship and say, "By the way, do you have a twin?"

—LARRY MILLER,
AMERICAN ACTOR

It's afterward you realize that the feeling of happiness you had with a man didn't necessarily prove that you loved him.

—MARGUERITE DURAS,
FRENCH WRITER

They spoil every romance by try-ing to make it last forever.

—OSCAR WILDE

Everyone deals with breakups dif-ferently. While some people sit at home crying into a teacup and drinking their own tears, others opt for more-productive coping methods. Like drowning their sorrows with drugs and alcohol, for example. True, it might not solve anything, but at least they'll run into plenty of people who are more pathetic than they are.

But whatever your coping mechanism of choice, it's impor-tant to get back out into the dat-ing world and remind yourself that not everybody is a lying, cheating dirtbag. It's just that the vast majority of people are.

It is foolish to tear

one's hair in grief,

as though sorrow

would be made less

by baldness.

—CICERO, ROMAN PHILOSOPHER

What a lovely surprise to finally discover how unlonely being alone can be.

—ELLEN BURSTYN,
AMERICAN ACTRESS

I love men, even though they're lying, cheating scumbags.

—GWYNETH PALTROW,
AMERICAN ACTRESS

The supply of good women far exceeds that of the men who deserve them.

—ROBERT GRAVES,
BRITISH POET AND NOVELIST

And I shall find some girl perhaps, and a better one than you, With eyes as wise, but kindlier, and lips as soft, but true, and I daresay she will do.

—RUPERT BROOKE,
BRITISH POET, "THE CHILTERNS"

Chapter 19

Marriage

When you date someone so long that you forget what you like about your partner, you have two options: Give up or get married. One might think the first option is the obvious choice, but there are a number of variables to consider.

First and foremost, age. Trading up might be a viable option in your twenties, but that prospect is less likely when you have more hair on your knuckles than on your head. Second, while you may not like your partner anymore, do you *dislike* him or her? You'd be surprised how many successful marriages are built on mutual indifference. Finally, do you have anything better to do with your time?

True, this hypothetical scenario paints a fairly grim picture of marriage, but I'd be doing you a disservice if I painted marriage as a lifetime of Eskimo kisses and breakfast in bed. As any married person will tell you, matrimony has its perks, but they are few and far between.

While you could take my word for it, there are plenty of a**holes more knowledgeable than I who can attest to the trials and tribulations of married life.

Marriage: A legal or religious ceremony by which two persons of the opposite sex solemnly agree to harass and spy on each other for ninety-nine years, or until death do them join.

—ELBERT HUBBARD,
AMERICAN WRITER

You're the reason our kids are so ugly.

—GROUCHO MARX

Bachelors know more about women than married men; if they didn't, they'd be married, too.

—H. L. MENCKEN,
AMERICAN JOURNALIST

The secret of a happy marriage remains a secret.

—HENNY YOUNGMAN,
BRITISH COMEDIAN

We are gonna have tons and tons of opportunities to meet gorgeous ladies that get so aroused by the thought of marriage that they'll throw their inhibitions to the wind.

—JEREMY GREY,
WEDDING CRASHERS

Men who have pierced ears are better prepared for marriage. They've experienced pain and bought jewelry.

—RITA RUDNER, AMERICAN
ACTRESS AND COMEDIAN

A man in love is incomplete until he has married. Then he's finished.

—ZSA ZSA GABOR

No married man is genuinely happy if he has to drink worse whisky than he used to drink when he was single.

—H. L. MENCKEN,
AMERICAN JOURNALIST

Since so many millions of people get married every year, it stands to reason that there must be some practical benefit to the tradition. A thorough investigation into the matter reveals the following results: You pay less in taxes.

There are a few smaller fringe benefits of matrimony, like the ability to fart in front of one another without apologizing or riding in the carpool lane whenever you want. But for the most part, marriage is about as fun as playing Hungry Hungry Hippos by yourself. Which might explain why so many people advise so strongly against it.

I am is reportedly the shortest sentence in the English language. Could it be that *I do* is the longest sentence?

—GEORGE CARLIN,
AMERICAN COMEDIAN

I was married by a judge. I should have asked for a jury.

—GROUCHO MARX

My wife converted me to religion. I never believed in hell until I married her.

—HAL ROACH,
AMERICAN DIRECTOR

My wife has a slight impediment in her speech—every now and then she stops to breathe.

—JIMMY DURANTE, AMERICAN
ACTOR AND MUSICIAN

When a man opens the car door for his wife, it's either a new car or a new wife.

—PRINCE PHILIP

A man's wife has more power over him than the state has.

—RALPH WALDO EMERSON

Some stuff does bother me about being married ... like having a husband.

—ROSEANNE BARR

I respect a woman too much to marry her.

—SYLVESTER STALLONE,
AMERICAN ACTOR

The tragedy is not

that love doesn't last.

The tragedy is the

love that lasts.

—SHIRLEY HAZZARD,
AUSTRALIAN AUTHOR

Women are
like elephants
to me: nice to
look at, but
I wouldn't
want to own
one.

—W. C. FIELDS,
AMERICAN COMEDIAN

If you have ever taken a bite of a sandwich and thought, *Man, this is the worst sandwich I have ever tasted. I need to share this horrible experience with everyone I know,* then you have some notion of what it's like to be married.

Based on everything we know about marriage, the logical conclusion would be that it would have ceased to exist by now. Yet marriage as an institution is stronger than ever. So much so that gay-rights activists are fighting to be just as miserable as their heterosexual peers. While nobody can be certain why we flock to the institution of marriage, a few forward-thinking souls certainly did their best to try and steer us away.

The dread of loneliness is greater than the dread of bondage, so we get married.

—CYRIL CONNOLLY,
BRITISH AUTHOR

Any intelligent woman who reads the marriage contract, and then goes into it, deserves all the consequences.

—ISADORA DUNCAN,
AMERICAN DANCER

Love is temporary insanity curable by marriage.

—AMBROSE BIERCE, AMERICAN
WRITER AND AUTHOR OF
THE DEVIL'S DICTIONARY

It is most unwise for people in love to marry.

—GEORGE BERNARD SHAW,
IRISH PLAYWRIGHT AND AUTHOR

Music played at weddings always reminds me of the music played for soldiers before they go into battle.

—HEINRICH HEINE,
GERMAN POET

I would rather be a beggar and single than a queen and married.

—ELIZABETH I

Marriage has no guarantees. If that's what you're looking for, go live with a car battery.

—ERMA BOMBECK,
AMERICAN HUMORIST

Getting married for sex is like buying a 747 for the free peanuts.

—JEFF FOXWORTHY,
AMERICAN COMEDIAN

After marriage, husband and wife become two sides of a coin; they just can't face each other, but still they stay together.

—HEMANT JOSHI, INDIAN
COMMUNICATIONS PROFESSOR

While it's true that nearly 50 percent of all marriages end in failure, that leaves slightly more than half of the married population who is potentially happy. Subtract from that number the roughly 75 percent who are just holding out for something better, and you've still got a decent chunk of people who aren't completely miserable with their partners. While that's not the most uplifting statistic ever compiled (or the most accurate), it is comforting to know that there are tens of couples out there who are actually perfect for one another.

An archaeologist is the best husband a woman can have. The older she gets, the more interested he is in her.

—AGATHA CHRISTIE

I'd never be unfaithful to my wife for the reason that I love my house very much.

—BOB MONKHOUSE,
BRITISH COMEDIAN AND ACTOR

Some people ask the secret of our long marriage. We take time to go to a restaurant two times a week. A little candlelight, dinner, soft music, and dancing. She goes Tuesdays; I go Fridays.

—HENNY YOUNGMAN,
BRITISH COMEDIAN

Only two things are necessary to keep one's wife happy. One is to let her think she is having her own way, and the other is to let her have it.

—LYNDON B. JOHNSON

I first learned the concepts of nonviolence in my marriage.

—MAHATMA GANDHI

Your idea of romance is popping the can away from my face.

—ROSEANNE BARR

Thanks to overexposure to fairy tales as children, many of us grow up thinking that we will wind up marrying a prince or a princess and live happily ever after. As time goes on, we decide we could settle for a famous actor or athlete. We eventually lower our expectations to include anyone with a college degree and all of his or her adult teeth. If only our parents had read us classified ads instead of fairy tales, we might have been better prepared for our inevitable fate.

It's a funny thing that when a man hasn't anything on earth to worry about, he goes off and gets married.

—ROBERT FROST

By all means marry; if you get a good wife, you'll be happy; if you get a bad one, you'll become a philosopher.

—SOCRATES

It is great to be a blonde. With low expectations it's very easy to surprise people.

—PAMELA ANDERSON,
AMERICAN ACTRESS AND MODEL

Everyone knows that a man can always marry even if he reaches 102, is penniless, and has all his faculties gone. There is always some woman willing to take a chance on him.

—AMY VANDERBILT, AMERICAN
AUTHOR AND AUTHORITY ON
ETIQUETTE

I have my standards. They may be low, but I have them.

—BETTE MIDLER

The difference between courtship and marriage is the difference between the pictures in a seed catalog and what comes up.

—JAMES WHARTON,
U.S. CONGRESSMAN

It's like cuddling with a Butterball turkey.

—JEFF FOXWORTHY,
AMERICAN COMEDIAN

Behind every great man, there is a surprised woman.

—MARYON PEARSON,
WIFE OF THE 14TH CANADIAN
PRIME MINISTER

Love isn't finding a perfect person. It's seeing an imperfect person perfectly.

—SAM KEEN, AMERICAN
AUTHOR AND PROFESSOR

The secret to a healthy marriage isn't trust or understanding. It isn't compromise and it isn't honesty. It's manipulation.

From the moment you say, "I do," until one of you dies or you get sick of each other (whichever comes first), you are stuck with this person. The only way to make the situation bearable is to gradually mold him or her into whatever image you have of the ideal spouse. Although you could sit down and talk through your problems, the far better approach is through subtle treachery. If you do it right, your spouse won't realize you've done anything at all.

The best way to get most husbands to do something is to suggest that perhaps they're too old to do it.

—ANNE BANCROFT,
AMERICAN ACTRESS

Honesty is the key to a relationship. If you can fake that, you're in.

—RICHARD JENI,
AMERICAN COMEDIAN AND ACTOR

When you see a married couple coming down the street, the one who is two or three steps ahead is the one that's mad.

—HELEN ROWLAND,
AMERICAN JOURNALIST

A husband is what

is left of the lover

after the nerve is

extracted.

—HELEN ROWLAND,
AMERICAN JOURNALIST

The only time a woman really succeeds in changing a man is when he is a baby.

—NATALIE WOOD

I love being married. It's so great to find that one special person you want to annoy for the rest of your life.

—RITA RUDNER, AMERICAN
ACTRESS AND COMEDIAN

While the beginning of a marriage is an exciting combination of playing house and seeing how many different surfaces you can comfortably do each other on, that honeymoon period generally fizzles out within about seventy-two hours. Now what?

Although some couples try to spice things up with clever distractions like children and funny costumes, the far better approach is to simply embrace the inevitable lameness. There's a certain soothing comfort in knowing that every Tuesday will be meatloaf night and every Thursday you'll play Othello.

My mother once told me that if a married couple puts a penny in a pot for every time they make love in the first year, and takes a penny out every time after that, they'll never get all the pennies out of the pot.

—ARMISTEAD MAUPIN,
AMERICAN AUTHOR

Do you know what it means to come home at night to a woman who'll give you a little love, a little affection, a little tenderness? It means you're in the wrong house.

—HENNY YOUNGMAN,
BRITISH COMEDIAN

Women speak because they wish to speak, whereas a man speaks only when driven to speech by something outside himself—like, for instance, he can't find any clean socks.

—JEAN KERR, AMERICAN
AUTHOR AND PLAYWRIGHT

My wife and I tried

to breakfast together,

but we had to stop or

our marriage would

have been wrecked.

—WINSTON CHURCHILL

Getting married is a lot like getting into a tub of hot water. After you get used to it, it ain't so hot.

—MINNIE PEARL,
AMERICAN ACTRESS

I married beneath me; all women do.

—NANCY ASTOR,
BRITISH POLITICIAN

The total amount of undesired sex endured by women is probably greater in marriage than in prostitution.

—BERTRAND RUSSELL,
BRITISH PHILOSOPHER

Afterword

After reading this compendium of important things said by notable a**holes throughout history, you can likely draw some conclusions:

- A**holes will always love to hear themselves talk.
- Earth will run out of many things: trees, oil, breathable air. But never a**holes.

The first is a given. Simply belly up to the bar at your local watering hole and even amateur a**holes will gladly talk your ear off about everything from what a shitty job the president is doing to how awful it is living with an incurable rash.

While the second observation may, at first, be disheartening, it's a fact you would do well to accept. You may have initially thought that a**holes may someday be weeded out through selective breeding or intense hypnosis, but it's time to accept that there is absolutely no hope for their eradication. And, as you've likely realized by now, that's not necessarily a bad thing.

Think about it; history's a**holes have done you a great service. For starters, they make you look like an all-around nice person. And, if you're standing behind an a**hole in line for your morning coffee, chances are, the barista will take extra care to get your coffee order right. Finally, and let's be honest about this one, those a**holes have the balls to actually say the stuff that you're thinking but are afraid to put out there—and for that we owe them our thanks.

So before we finish our exploration into all things a**hole, I want to leave you with a few final musings from history's greatest wordsmiths. After all, who can say it better than they can.

Only two things are infinite, the universe and human stupidity, and I'm not sure about the former.

—ALBERT EINSTEIN

What do you call love, hate, charity, revenge, humanity, magnanimity, forgiveness? Different results of the one master impulse: the necessity of securing one's self-approval.

—MARK TWAIN

He can compress the most words into the smallest idea of any man I know.

—ABRAHAM LINCOLN

You can only be young once. But you can always be immature.

—DAVE BARRY, AMERICAN AUTHOR AND COLUMNIST

We must laugh at man to avoid crying for him.

—NAPOLEON BONAPARTE

Nobody's perfect. Well, there was this one guy, but we killed him. . . .

—CHRISTOPHER MOORE, AMERICAN AUTHOR

Blessed is the man who, having nothing to say, abstains from giving us wordy evidence of the fact.

—GEORGE ELLIOT, BRITISH NOVELIST

Tragedy is when I cut my finger. Comedy is when you fall into an open sewer and die.

—MEL BROOKS,
AMERICAN COMEDIAN,
DIRECTOR, AND ACTOR

If there is anything the non-conformist hates worse than a conformist, it's another nonconformist who doesn't conform to the prevailing standard of nonconformity.

—BILL VAUGHAN,
AMERICAN COLUMNIST

A child of five would understand this. Send someone to fetch a child of five.

—GROUCHO MARX

You take care and I hope I'll run into you—when I'm driving.

—RODNEY DANGERFIELD,
AMERICAN COMEDIAN

Words are, of course, the most powerful drug used by mankind.

—RUDYARD KIPLING

You can't imagine what a pleasure this complete laziness is to me: not a thought in my brain—you might send a ball rolling through it!

—LEO TOLSTOY

Some days even my lucky rocket-ship underpants won't help.

—CALVIN, *CALVIN AND HOBBES*

First secure an independent income, then practice virtue.

—GREEK PROVERB

The best measure of a man's honesty isn't his income tax return. It's the zero adjust on his bathroom scale.

—ARTHUR C. CLARKE, BRITISH
SCIENCE-FICTION AUTHOR

If they can make penicillin out of moldy bread, they can sure make something out of you.

—MUHAMMAD ALI

Never attribute to malice what can be adequately explained by stupidity.

—NICK DIAMOS, AMERICAN AUTHOR

If my critics saw me walking over the Thames, they would say it was because I couldn't swim.

—MARGARET THATCHER

If you want to kill any idea in the world, get a committee working on it.

—CHARLES F. KETTERING, AMERICAN INVENTOR

One picture is worth 1,000 denials.

—RONALD REAGAN

Do you suppose I could buy back my introduction to you?

—GROUCHO MARX

Every time I think that I'm getting old, and gradually going to the grave, something else happens.

—ELVIS PRESLEY

If this is tea, please bring me some coffee . . . but if this is coffee, please bring me some tea.

—ABRAHAM LINCOLN

Shoving feathers in your ass does not make you a chicken.

—BRAD PITT

I trust no one. Not even myself

—JOSEPH STALIN

I've developed a new philosophy . . . I only dread one day at a time.

—CHARLES SCHULZ

I do not consider it an insult but rather a compliment to be called an agnostic. I do not pretend to know where many ignorant men are sure—that is all that agnosticism means.

—CLARENCE SEWARD DARROW, AMERICAN LAWYER FAMOUS FOR HIS DEFENSE OF JOHN T. SCOPES IN THE "SCOPES MONKEY TRIAL"

If you can't be kind, at least be vague.

—DAVID POWERS, SPECIAL ASSISTANT TO JOHN F. KENNEDY

Man is the most intelligent of the animals—and the most silly.

—DIOGENES, GREEK EXPLORER

A common mistake that people make when trying to design something completely foolproof is to underestimate the ingenuity of complete fools.

—DOUGLAS ADAMS, BRITISH WRITER AND AUTHOR OF *THE HITCHHIKER'S GUIDE TO THE GALAXY*

A humanitarian is always a hypocrite.

—GEORGE ORWELL, ENGLISH AUTHOR AND JOURNALIST

To be stupid, selfish, and have good health are three requirements for happiness, though if stupidity is lacking, all is lost.

—GUSTAVE FLAUBERT, FRENCH WRITER

I guess I just prefer to see the dark side of things. The glass is always half empty. And cracked. And I just cut my lip on it. And chipped a tooth.

—JANEANE GAROFALO, AMERICAN COMEDIAN AND ACTRESS

Go to Heaven for the climate, Hell for the company.

—MARK TWAIN

I am free of all prejudices. I hate everyone equally.

—W. C. FIELDS

She had a pretty gift for quotation, which is a serviceable substitute for wit.

—W. SOMERSET MAUGHAM,
BRITISH PLAYWRIGHT

Some scientists claim that hydrogen, because it is so plentiful, is the basic building block of the universe. I dispute that. I say there is more stupidity than hydrogen, and that is the basic building block of the universe.

—FRANK ZAPPA,
AMERICAN ROCK MUSICIAN

If it turns out that there is a God, I don't think that he's evil. But the worst that you can say about him is that basically he's an underachiever.

—WOODY ALLEN

Only the mediocre are always at their best.

—JEAN GIRAUDOUX,
FRENCH WRITER

The only reason bad things happen to you is because you're a dumbass.

—RED FORMAN,
THAT 70'S SHOW

Death is the solution to all problems. No man—no problem.

—JOSEPH STALIN

THE QUOTABLE A**HOLE

A witty saying proves

nothing.

—Voltaire,
French philosopher

If there is anyone here whom I have not insulted, I beg his pardon.

—Johannes Brahms,
German composer

So now that you've been educated in the art of a**holes, go out and use their words to put others in their place—or just mutter them under your breath when you run into one of them. The choice is yours!

But now I leave you with these invaluable words from British actor George Sanders, "Goodbye. I am leaving because I am bored."

INDEX

Bok, Derek, 91
Bombeck, Erma, 7, 8, 10, 59, 144, 222
Bonaparte, Napoleon, 163, 167, 228
Bonta, Vanna, 164
Boosler, Elayne, 146, 208
Borge, Victor, 5, 211
Börne, Karl Ludwig, 139
Bowles, Lester, 172
Boy George, 41
Brahms, Johannes, 233
Brault, Robert, 95
Brecher, Irving, 43
Brecht, Bertolt, 18
Brenner, David, 203
Brent, David, 90, 96, 105, 110, 111
Brett, George, 155
Brillat-Savarin, Jean Anthelme, 54
Brilliant, Ashleigh, 4, 5, 15, 142, 189, 209
Brin, David, 139
Brinkley, David, 144
Brisbane, Arthur, 22
Brockman, Kent, 117
Brooke, Rupert, 216
Brooks, Mel, 229
Brophy, Brigid, 126
Broun, Heywood, 82, 152
Brown, Alan Whitney, 162
Brown, James, 133
Brown, Les, 199
Brown, Rita Mae, 80
Brown, Sarah, 108
Browne, Thomas, 125
Buckley, William F., Jr., 35
Buddha, 42, 205
Buffett, Warren, 78, 173
Burke, Edmund, 136
Burnham, Lester, 110
Burns, Frank, 167
Burns, George, 4, 50, 122, 124, 136
Burstyn, Ellen, 215
Bush, Barbara, 187

Bush, George W., 33, 162, 168
Butler, Rhett, 137
Butler, Samuel, 8, 80, 127
Byrne, Robert, 159, 173
Byron, Lord, 13

Cain, Dean, 210
Calvin (*Calvin and Hobbes*), 38, 44, 90, 93, 191, 229
Camus, Albert, 105
Capone, Al, 137
Carey, Drew, 105, 202
Carlin, George, 24, 58, 59, 64, 76, 114, 136, 168, 219
Carnegie, Andrew, 129
Carnegie, Dale, 30
Carr, Jimmy, 30
Carrie (*Sex and the City*), 208
Carroll, Jonathan, 186
Carter, Billy, 59
Carville, James, 132
Castro, Rosalia de, 55
Catherine the Great, 142
Caulfield, Holden, 28
Cavett, Dick, 103
Cavour, Camillo di, 180
Cervantes, Miguel de, 130
Chandler, Raymond, 51, 191
Chanel, Coco, 18
Charles, Count Talleyrand, 204
Cher, 191, 211
Chesterfield, Lord, 21
Chesterton, G. K., 166
Chinese proverb, 14
Christie, Agatha, 93, 127, 222
Chrysler, Walter, 108
Churchill, Winston, 47, 51, 81, 142, 153, 165, 226
Ciardi, John, 100
Cicero, 215
Clark, Dick, 12
Clark, Richard, 65
Clarke, Arthur C., 229

War, 161–70
Warhol, Andy, 65
Washington, George, 167
Wayne, John, 20, 43, 138
Weaver, Earl, 158
Weiler, A. H., 109
Wellesley, Arthur, 163
Welsh, Irvine, 67
Wesley (*The Princess Bride*), 30
West, Mae, 23, 197, 199, 212
Wharton, Edith, 125
Wharton, James, 224
White, Slappy, 117
Whitehead, Alfred North, 31
Whitehorn, Katharine, 71, 128
Whitton, Charlotte, 98
Wholey, Dennis, 44
Wilde, Oscar, 4, 22, 50, 77, 80, 92, 94, 152, 192, 194, 197, 204, 208, 215
Wilhelm, Kaiser, 52
Will, George, 152
Williams, Lee Fox, 100
Williams, Pat, 158
Williams, Robin, 61, 67, 203, 214
Williams, Tennessee, 124
Wilmot, John, 11
Wilson, Earl, 84, 131, 144
Winchell, Walter, 205
Winfrey, Oprah, 189
Winnie the Pooh, 35, 38
Wohford, Jim, 150
Wood, Natalie, 225
Woollcott, Alexander, 80
WOPR (War Operation Plan Response), 151
Working, 87–111
Wormer, Dean Vernon, 52
Worthington, Michael, 119
Wright, Steven, 37, 84, 124, 141, 153

Yamada, Masahiro, 114
Yasenek, Rene, 187
Youngman, Henny, 19, 37, 53, 117, 126, 132, 212, 218, 222, 226

Zappa, Frank, 51, 68, 232
Zevin, Dan, 90
Ziglar, Zig, 120
Zinn, Howard, 175

ABOUT THE AUTHOR

Eric Grzymkowski is a humor writer and aspiring a**hole. When not writing, he can be found flipping off unsuspecting motorists, cutting in line at the supermarket, and talking on his cell phone at the movies. He resides in Somerville, Massachusetts, where he spends the majority of his time searching for witty comebacks to use in obscure situations.

DAILY BENDER

Want Some More?

Hit up our humor blog, The Daily Bender, to get your fill of all things funny—be it subversive, odd, offbeat, or just plain mean. The Bender editors are there to get you through the day and on your way to happy hour. Whether we're linking to the latest video that made us laugh or calling out (or bullshit on) whatever's happening, we've got what you need for a good laugh.

If you like our book, you'll love our blog. (And if you hated it, "man up" and tell us why.) Visit The Daily Bender for a shot of humor that'll serve you until the bartender can.

Sign up for our newsletter at
www.adamsmedia.com/blog/humor
and download our Top Ten Maxims No Man Should Live Without.